Complete IELTS

Bands 6.5–7.5

Workbook *without Answers*

Rawdon Wyatt

Shaftesbury Road, Cambridge CB2 8EA, United Kingdom

One Liberty Plaza, 20th Floor, New York, NY 10006, USA

477 Williamstown Road, Port Melbourne, VIC 3207, Australia

314–321, 3rd Floor, Plot 3, Splendor Forum, Jasola District Centre, New Delhi – 110025, India

103 Penang Road, #05-06/07, Visioncrest Commercial, Singapore 238467

Cambridge University Press & Assessment is a department of the University of Cambridge.

We share the University's mission to contribute to society through the pursuit of education, learning and research at the highest international levels of excellence.

Information on this title: www.cambridge.org/9781009672191

© Cambridge University Press & Assessment 2013

This publication is in copyright. Subject to statutory exception and to the provisions of relevant collective licensing agreements, no reproduction of any part may take place without the written permission of Cambridge University Press & Assessment.

First published 2013
20 19 18 17 16 15 14 13 12 11 10 9 8 7 6 5 4 3 2

Printed in Great Britain by CPI Group (UK) Ltd, Croydon CR0 4YY

A catalogue record for this publication is available from the British Library

ISBN 978-1-009-68366-1 Student's Book with Answers
ISBN 978-1-009-68365-4 Student's Book without Answers
ISBN 978-1-107-60964-8 Teacher's Book
ISBN 978-1-009-67220-7 Workbook with Answers
ISBN 978-1-009-67219-1 Workbook without Answers

Additional resources for this publication at www.cambridge.org/elt/completeielts

Cambridge University Press & Assessment has no responsibility for the persistence or accuracy of URLs for external or third-party internet websites referred to in this publication, and does not guarantee that any content on such websites is, or will remain, accurate or appropriate. Information regarding prices, travel timetables, and other factual information given in this work is correct at the time of first printing but Cambridge University Press & Assessment does not guarantee the accuracy of such information thereafter.

Contents

Map of the units — 4

1 **Getting higher qualifications** — 6
2 **Colour my world** — 12
3 **A healthy life** — 18
4 **Art and the artist** — 24
5 **Stepping back in time** — 30
6 **IT society** — 36
7 **Our relationship with nature** — 42
8 **Across the universe** — 48

Recording scripts — 54
Answer key — 62

Acknowledgements — 71

Map of the units

Unit title	Reading	Listening
1 Getting higher qualifications	Reading: The University of Life • True / False / Not Given • Note completion • Short-answer questions	Listening: Voluntary work • Form completion
2 Colour my world	Reading: An invention to dye for: the colour purple • Matching headings • Pick from a list • Summary completion	Listening: Information on a new book • Table completion • Pick from a list
3 A healthy life	Reading: Scientific research reveals hidden benefits of regular exercise • Yes / No / Not Given • Summary completion with a box • Multiple choice	Listening: Two people talking about common painkillers • Matching • Flow-chart completion
4 Art and the artist	Reading: A brief history of photography in advertising • Table completion • Flow-chart completion • True / False / Not Given	Listening: A lecture on prehistoric visual art • Note completion
5 Stepping back in time	Reading: When and why did we learn to stand on our own two feet? • Matching information • Sentence completion • Matching features	Listening: Describing a talk by an archaeologist • Multiple choice • Note completion
6 IT society	Reading: How green is your PlanIT Valley? • Multiple choice • Yes / No / Not Given • Matching sentence endings	Listening: A lecture on internet banking • Note completion
7 Our relationship with nature	Reading: Keystone species • Matching headings • Sentence completion • Pick from a list	Listening: A student and tutor talking about bird watching • Sentence completion • Labelling a plan • Short-answer questions
8 Across the universe	Reading: Life on Mars? • Yes / No / Not Given • Multiple choice • Summary completion with a box	Listening: A lecture about health problems in space • Note completion

Writing	Vocabulary and Spelling	Grammar
Writing Task 1 • Writing an introduction to the task • Choosing the correct vocabulary to describe a graph	• Dependent prepositions • Key vocabulary	• *used to / would* • Superlative forms • Past simple, present perfect simple and past perfect simple
Writing Task 2 • Analysing the task and brainstorming ideas • Planning an answer	• Phrasal verbs • Key vocabulary	• Nouns and articles
Writing Task 1 • Summarising key features in more than one chart • Paragraphing and the overview • Using your own words • Expressing amount, extent or category	• Verb + noun collocations • Key vocabulary	• Expressing large and small differences
Writing Task 2 • Brainstorming main ideas • Maintaining a clear position • Using reasons and examples for support • Introducing arguments • Choosing the best conclusion	• Collocations and phrases with *make*, *take*, *do* and *have* • Key vocabulary	• Expressing purpose, cause and effect
Writing Task 1 • Summarising a diagram • Analysing the task and organising the answer • Linking information, signalling and comparing stages • Using participle clauses to express consequences	• Word formation – negative affixes • Key vocabulary	• Using sequencers • Speaking hypothetically
Writing Task 2 • Describing advantages and disadvantages • Structuring an answer and linking paragraphs • Presenting a balanced view: discourse markers	• Adjective + noun collocations • Key vocabulary	• Referencing
Writing Task 1 • Categorising data • Organising information • Proofing your work: punctuation	• Idiomatic expressions • Key vocabulary	• Speculating and talking about the future
Writing Task 2 • Linking ideas and views across paragraphs	• Verbs and dependent prepositions • Key vocabulary	• Emphasising

Unit 1 Getting higher qualifications

Listening   Part 1

1 Look at the advertisement on a college notice board. From the information in the advertisement, can you predict what you are going to hear?

Care for the Community

Part-time student volunteers wanted.

Can you spare a few hours each week to help out in your local community? We urgently need volunteers to help us run and support a range of local care services. We especially need people who can:

- offer care and assistance to the elderly

- help those with mobility problems

- provide support for young people from disadvantaged backgrounds.

For more information, visit www.care4thecommunity.co.uk

2 Look at the Exam task below and decide what sort of information you need to complete each gap.

Questions 1–12

Complete the form below.

*Write **NO MORE THAN THREE WORDS AND / OR A NUMBER** for each answer.*

Care for the Community

Applicant details

Name: 1 ....
Sex: Female

Occupation: 2 .... student at Brookfields University studying on 3 .... Course (BA).

Contact details

Phone: 4 ....
Email: 5 ....@chatbox.co.uk
Availability: Up to 6 .... per week.

Other information

- Reason for applying: Would like 7 ....

- Area of interest: Children with 8 ....

- Experience: Has recently done similar work at a 9 .... Found it 10 ....

- Perceived strengths: Has excellent 11 .... Also listens to people.

12 .... arranged for Wednesday 10th September.

3 🎧 Now listen and complete Questions 1–12.

4 Look carefully at your answers and check to make sure:

- you haven't exceeded the allowed number of words and/or numbers ☐
- your answer is grammatically correct (where relevant), and/or collocates with the words before or after the gap (especially in questions 7–12) ☐
- your spelling is correct. ☐

Vocabulary

Dependent prepositions

1 Complete each sentence with one word from the first box and one from the second box. Then write your answers in the crossword.

available	concentrate	confidence		for	in
deal	involved	participate	related	on	to
reputation	spent	suited		with	

1 The college currently has no money .... new computers, so we'll have to make the best of the old ones.

2 I'm interested in politics, but I don't think I would be .... a career in it.

3 I have complete .... my tutor when she says that she'll do her best to get us through our exams.

4 One thing I've learnt is never get .... an argument unless it affects you directly.

5 During tutorials, I always try to .... the discussion as much as possible.

6 Mr Wilkinson has a .... being the strictest tutor in the college.

7 A lot of student illnesses before exams are .... stress caused by overwork.

8 On average, just under a third of a student's income is .... accommodation.

9 I tend to .... problems one at a time rather than try to tackle them all at once.

10 The college library is always so noisy it's really difficult to .... your work.

Key vocabulary

2 Complete each gap in this passage with a word or words from the first box, and a word or words from the second box.

brings	channels all of its		desire	programme
common	get to		range	resources
go on	recruitment		people together	the top
vast	vocational		to do	training

For the last two years, I've been studying at the International University in Bampton, which I believe is one of the best universities in the country. As well as offering a **1** .... of academic courses, it also runs several **2** .... programmes, and is especially well-known for its computer-programming courses. What I like about it is that it is a truly international university which **3** .... from all around the world. It expects its students to be hardworking and to show initative, and it **4** .... into ensuring they get the best education possible. The students all have a **5** .... – to get top grades in their subjects – and many **6** .... postgraduate studies before taking their first step on the career ladder. Naturally, many expect to **7** .... in their chosen career. The university has an excellent reputation, and some of the world's biggest and most prestigious companies visit the college each year as part of their **8** ....

Getting higher qualifications 7

Reading Section 1

1 You are going to read a passage about gap years. Skim the passage. Which of these best describes the writer's purpose? Circle A, B or C.

A To summarise the main reasons why students take a gap year.
B To explain why some gap year programmes are so successful.
C To illustrate, with examples, one particular advantage of a gap year.

The University of Life

Katherine Demopoulos meets students who took a break from study to volunteer overseas and returned with a new sense of purpose

The majority of 18-year-old students entering higher education go straight from school to university. For many school leavers, however, there is the irresistible attraction of the 'gap year', a time between school and university when they decide to experience something new, different or exciting. Many of these so-called 'gappers' go off travelling around the world, often supplementing their limited funds by taking on casual work, while others may do voluntary work in a village in a distant part of the world.

For the majority of gappers, the gap year is simply a chance to enjoy life as an independent adult for the first time. Increasingly, however, they are also proving a great way of reinvigorating a lapsed or flagging interest in education, offering a chance to think about why you should study, or if you need to study at all. A growing number of students, having taken a break after school, are heading back into further and higher education via a roundabout route of working and 'gapping'. According to the latest data from the British university admissions service, UCAS, 105,000 students aged 19, and 44,400 aged 20, entered higher education last year – figures that show a steady annual increase in this age group over the previous three years.

19-year-old student Christine Samways is a typical example. She left school at 16 with nine good exam passes at grades A to C, but did not want to continue studying at the time. She was also worried that, despite having all the attributes of a good student, she would find the challenges of higher education too great and would be forced to drop out. Instead, she gained a vocational qualification in hairdressing. However, she very quickly began to realise it was not quite what she wanted and that going back into some kind of education could be her next step. Like many 16-year-old school leavers starting work for the first time, it dawned on her that if you don't have qualifications, or the right qualifications, you have fewer work choices. 'The things that you want to do just aren't available to you,' she says.

Unsure of what her next step should be, Christine decided to head to Mexico to do voluntary work at a children's home. She was there for a year under the auspices of the International Cultural Youth Exchange (ICYE) – an organisation which has been running since 1949, when it sent 50 German students to the US as peace ambassadors. She never expected that working in Mexico would give her such a sense of confidence and, perhaps just as importantly, direction. On returning home to the UK, she decided to make a fresh start in education by enrolling on a course in Social Sciences and Humanities to prepare herself for university. Her new sense of confidence helped at her college interview. Previously, a formal interview would have made her very nervous, but she now found it much easier to talk on an informal and formal level to people she didn't know. 'I feel more comfortable in these situations,' she says. 'Mexico was the first time I'd been out of my comfort zone. Now I think I can cope with things better.'

Christine is now working towards a degree in International Development at Bath University, a choice of subject informed by her experience of working with Mexican children. And, as well as finding some direction in her career, she now speaks good Spanish – a skill she says she intends to keep up, perhaps by working abroad. She knows that the Mexican children's home benefited from her time there, just as she did. As well as being 'an extra pair of hands', she helped to streamline the children's timetable so they spent more structured time on homework. The children began to 'do better in school,' she says. 'You only move up a year if you pass a year – I got four children that at the beginning of the year were told they were going to stay down, but they moved up. It's a good feeling.'

ICYE also brings students to Europe from the countries that European students traditionally visit. Agnes Eldad, from Kampala, Uganda, has just graduated with a degree in Social Work. She came to the UK in January this year, getting a voluntary work placement relieving full-time carers of elderly people in Bexleyheath, Kent. With her social work background, she wanted to understand how elderly people were treated in Britain and to see for herself how their relationships with their children, grandchildren and in-laws worked.

Agnes found the experience extremely beneficial, but says that the ICYE only really works if participants have a focus for what they want to do, see and study. Ironically, for her, this could be the only chance to work with elderly people before she goes back home in January. In Uganda, old people live with, and are supported by, their families, so she won't have an opportunity to work with them. Instead, she now wants to set up her own vocational training programme for young girls in northern Uganda. Agnes says her time in the UK has helped her to set her goals for the future.

❷ Now look at Questions 1–13 below and underline the key words and phrases. Then read the passage and answer the questions.

Questions 1–5

Do the following statements agree with the information in the Reading passage?

Write:

TRUE if the statement agrees with the information

FALSE if the statement contradicts the information

NOT GIVEN if there is no information on this

1 The majority of young people who go travelling during their gap year must work in order to finance their trip. ....

2 Taking a gap year can give young people time to consider whether or not they want to continue with their studies. ....

3 The number of university students has increased in the last few years. ....

4 Christine Samways lacks the right qualities to be a good student. ....

5 Christine Samways believes that if you lack educational qualifications, your career options are reduced. ....

Questions 6–10

Complete the notes below.

*Choose **NO MORE THAN TWO WORDS** from the passage for each answer.*

<u>Christine Samways: ICYE participant</u>

Carried out **6** .... in Mexico.

Programme gave her more **7** .... in herself.

Returned to **8** .... when she was back in the UK.

Currently studying **9** ....

Thinks that **10** .... may be a good way of maintaining her Spanish.

Questions 11–13

Answer the questions below.

*Choose **NO MORE THAN TWO WORDS** from the passage for each answer.*

11 According to Agnes Eldad, what do people need in order to benefit from an ICYE exchange programme? ....

12 Who does Agnes Eldad plan to work with when she finishes her ICYE programme?
....

13 What does Agnes Eldad have now that she didn't have before she came to the UK?
....

❸ Review your answers. For Questions 6–13, make sure that you have not used more than the maximum allowed number of words.

Grammar

used to / would

▶ Student's Book, page 120

① Complete the passage with expressions from the box. Use each expression once only.

~~didn't use to be~~	used to be spent	used to pour
used to seeing	used to have	would arrive
would go off	would have to	would receive
wouldn't go		

Today, the Park Street Academy is widely recognised as being one of the best colleges in the country. However, it **1** ..*didn't use to be*.. like this. In fact, it **2** .... a very bad reputation. Students **3** .... late, and often they **4** .... to classes at all. The college building was in a terrible state. When it rained, water **5** .... through holes in the ceiling and the power **6** .... suddenly without any reason. In winter, the rooms were so cold that you quickly became **7** .... people in classrooms wrapped up like they were in the Arctic.

Then, in 2010, a new head teacher was appointed, and she turned the place around. Strict discipline was applied at all levels. For example, students who were late or absent without reason **8** .... pay a financial penalty, while those who improved their academic record **9** .... rewards in the form of things like cinema tickets. Meanwhile, money that **10** .... on unimportant things like computer games for the library was instead used to repair the building.

Superlative forms

▶ Student's Book, page 119

② Underline the correct words or phrases in bold in these sentences.

1 My second **more favourite / favourite** subject was Art.

2 My Maths teacher Mrs Jennings was **the least popular / less popular** teacher in the school.

3 My English teacher, Mr Clark, was one of the **most funny / funniest** teachers I have ever had.

4 Mr Clark probably had the **lowest / most low** rate of absenteeism in the school.

5 When he ran the school's drama club, it had the **greatest number / most number** of members in its history.

6 It was the **greatest popular / most popular** activity by far.

Past simple, present perfect simple and past perfect simple

③ Complete this passage with the correct form of the verbs in brackets.

Since it first opened in 1989, St Darren's College **1** ..*has had*.. (have) a chequered history. The first five years **2** .... (be) slow in terms of student numbers, but after they **3** .... (receive) an excellent report in 1994, the number of students applying to the college **4** .... (rise), and **5** .... (continue) to do so each year for the next eight years. However, in 2002, the college **6** .... (see) a 30% increase in rent. Nobody at the college **7** .... (predict) this, and they **8** .... (have to) increase fees. As a result, in 2003, student numbers, which **9** .... (rise) consistently each year since 1994, suddenly **10** .... (stagnate). They then **11** .... (start) to fall. By 2007, student numbers **12** .... (fall) to less than 100. The following year, with applications at an all time low, the college **13** .... (shut) down. In 2010, the local council **14** .... (take) over the buildings, and **15** .... (start) offering vocational courses. Since then, St Darren's College **16** .... (go) from strength to strength.

Writing Task 1

❶ Look at the graph below and complete this introductory sentence by arranging the expressions in the box.

| did over a | school leavers | three things that |
| five-year period | information about | |

The graph gives ....

....

The graph below gives the results of a survey showing what 1,000 young people did after leaving school between 2008 and 2012.

Summarise the information by selecting and reporting the main features, and make comparisons where relevant.

School leavers 2008–2012

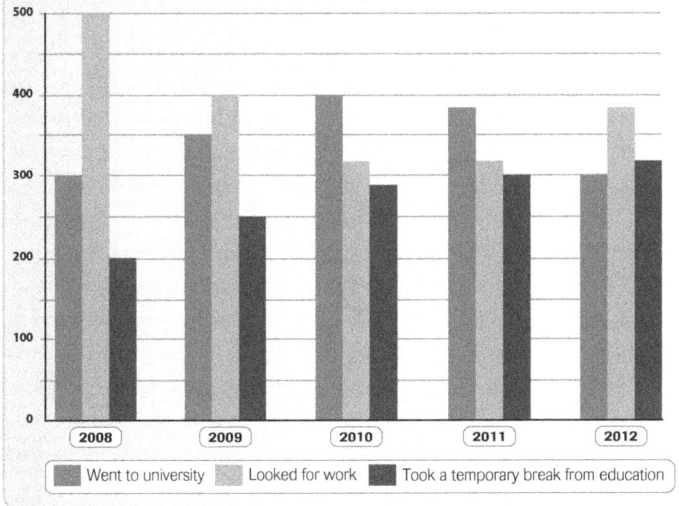

❷ Complete the rest of the answer with words and phrases from the box.

by just over	by the same amount
continuous and steady	differences	less marked
more detailed	most noticeable	fluctuated
significant changes	stagnating	the same

At the beginning of the five-year period, about half of the school leavers surveyed looked for work. Of the remaining 500, 300 went to university and 200 took a temporary break from their education. By the end of the five years, however, the figures for those seeking employment and for those taking a break from their education had seen **1** .... The former had fallen **2** .... a hundred, while the latter had risen **3** .... Meanwhile, the number of school leavers going to university was

4 .... as it had been at the beginning of the period. Overall, the **5** .... between the three groups had become **6** ....

A **7** .... look at the graph reveals that the number of school leavers going to university and the number of leavers looking for work **8** .... Between 2008 and 2010, the former increased while the latter decreased. Then in 2011 and 2012, the number of those going to university fell, while after **9** .... briefly in 2011, the number of those looking for employment rose. The number of school leavers taking a break from their education saw a **10** .... rise.

Overall, the **11** .... changes involved the number of school leavers looking for work and those taking a break from education. This shows that more young people planned to enter higher education, even though they decided to wait a while before doing so.

❸ Now write your answer to this Writing task in about 20 minutes. Your answer should be at least 150 words long.

The graph below shows the percentage change in places where students lived over five decades.

Summarise the information by selecting and reporting the main features, and make comparisons where relevant.

Types of student accommodation, 1960s–2000s.

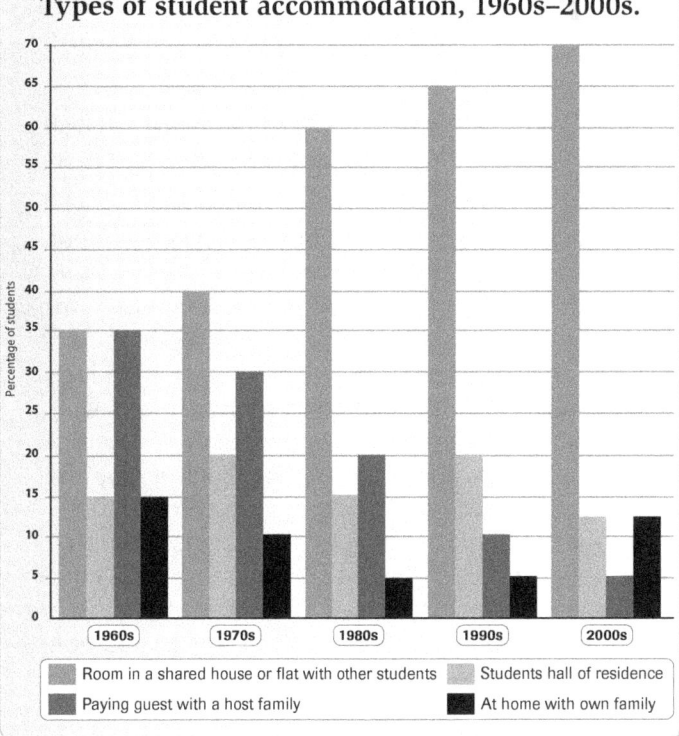

Getting higher qualifications

Unit 2 Colour my world

Reading   Section 2

1 Quickly read the passage below, which is about the colour purple. Match the names of the people (1–6) with the thing they do or did (a–e). There is one person who does not match any of the letters.

1 William Perkin
2 August Wilhelm von Hofmann
3 Simon Garfield
4 Queen Victoria
5 Dr Max Luscher
6 Julia Kubler

a believed that colours could be used to treat illnesses
b wrote a biography about an historical figure
c uses colours as a form of alternative medicine
d invented an artificial dye
e taught chemistry

An invention to dye for: the colour purple

A 19th century research chemist was trying to make medicine when, instead, he came up with a coloured dye that has ensured the world is a brighter place.

A Of all the colours, purple has perhaps the most powerful connotations. From the earliest cultures to the present day, people have sought to harness its visual power to mark themselves out as better than those around them. From bishops to kings, pop stars to fashion models, its wearing has been a calculated act of showing off. In ancient Rome, for example, purple was such a revered colour that only the emperor was allowed to wear it. Indeed, an emperor who was referred to as *porphyrogenitus*, ('born to the purple') was especially important, since this meant that he had inherited his position through family connections rather than seizing power through military force.

B But why purple? At that time, purple dye was an expensive substance produced in a complicated, foul-smelling and time-consuming process. This involved boiling thousands of molluscs in water in order to harvest their glandular juices. The technique had originally been developed by the Phoenicians over a thousand years previously, and it hadn't changed since. Cheaper but poorer quality purple dyes could be made from lichens using an equally messy and unpleasant procedure, but they were not as bright, and the colour quickly faded. It was no surprise, therefore, that good purple dye was a rare and precious thing, and clothes dyed purple were beyond the financial means of most people.

C However, times have changed. In the great consumer democracy of the 21st century, even the most humble citizen can choose it as the colour of their latest outfit. For that privilege, we must thank a young 19th century research chemist, William Perkin. A talented 15-year-old when he entered the Royal College of Chemistry in London in 1853, Perkin was immediately appointed as laboratory assistant to his tutor, August Wilhelm von Hofmann. He became determined to prove Hofmann's claim that quinine, a drug used to treat fevers such as malaria, could be synthesised in a laboratory. However, rather than the cure desperately needed for people dying from malaria in tropical countries, he produced little more than a black, sticky mess that turned purple when dissolved in industrial alcohol. Perkin's experiments could have been a complete waste of time, but to his surprise and, ultimately, financial benefit, his purple liquid turned out to be a long-lasting dye that was to transform fashion.

D Perkin repeated his experiments in an improvised laboratory in his garden shed, perfecting the process for making the substance he had called mauveine after the French mallow plant. It was, says Simon Garfield, the author of *Mauve* which details Perkin's life and work, an astonishing breakthrough. 'Once you could do that you could make colour in a factory from chemicals rather than insects or plants. It opened up the prospect of mass-produced artificial dyes and made Perkin one of the first scientists to bridge the gap between pure chemistry and its industrial applications.' It didn't take long for the chemist, still only 18, to capitalise on his creation, patenting the product, convincing his father and brother to back it with savings, and finding a manufacturer who could help him bring it rapidly to the market. The buying public loved it, and clothes coloured with purple started appearing in shops up and down the country.

Appropriately, considering the origins of Perkins' colour, he was to receive a helping hand from the two most important women of the day. Queen Victoria caused a sensation when she stepped out at the Royal Exhibition in 1862 wearing a silk gown dyed with mauveine. In Paris, Napoleon III's wife, Empress Eugenie, amazed the court when she was seen wearing it. To propel the scientist further on the way to a great fortune, the fashion of the time was for broad skirts that, happily for him, needed a lot of his revolutionary new dye.

E Perkins, ever the serious scientist, would have been among the first to point out that his mauve is just one of a range of colours described in everyday language as purple. Not itself a true colour of the spectrum – that position is given to indigo and violet – purple normally refers to those colours which inhabit the limits of human perception in the area between red and violet. Newton excluded the colour from his colour wheel. Scientists today talk about the 'line of purples' which include violet, mauve, magenta, indigo and lilac.

F In the alternative medical practice of colour therapy, which practitioners say can trace its origins back to ancient India, the 'purple range' colours of indigo and violet are vital. They refer to spiritual energy centres known as chakras and are situated in the head. The colours and their 'medical' qualities were first officially listed by the Swiss scientist Dr Max Luscher, who said that appropriately coloured lights, applied to specific chakras, could treat ailments from depression to grief. Julia Kubler is one of Britain's leading colour therapists and has been using colours to treat patients at her clinic at Manningtree, Essex, for 15 years. Purple, she says, 'is consistent with intuition and higher understanding, with spirituality and meditation. It combines the coolness of blue with a bit of red that makes it not just passive but active.'

It is hardly the most outlandish of claims for this most enigmatic of colours. Variously touted as the colour of everything from insanity to equality, it is enjoying a new role as the symbol of political compromise. Purple may have had its origins in the ancient world, but thanks to a young chemist, it still has a brilliant future.

❷ **Look at Questions 1–14 below, and underline the key words and phrases. Then look for the answers in the passage.**

Questions 1–6

The reading passage has six sections, **A–F**.

Choose the correct heading for each section from the list of headings below.

List of headings	
i	From the laboratory to the High Street
ii	Seeking royal support
iii	An unexpected but fortunate side result
iv	The healing power of purple
v	An old problem
vi	Standing out from the crowd
vii	Finding an alternative cure for a common illness
viii	Part of a larger family
ix	An ancient manufacturing practice

1 Section A ....   4 Section D ....
2 Section B ....   5 Section E ....
3 Section C ....   6 Section F ....

Colour my world

Questions 7–10

Choose **TWO** *letters, A–E.*

Questions 7–8

What **TWO** *points does the writer make about the colour purple and purple dye before William Perkin's creation?*

A It was only used to colour clothes.
B It was originally produced for Roman emperors.
C It was not easy to make.
D There were many different techniques used to make it.
E Some purple dyes were inferior to others.

Questions 9–10

What **TWO** *things about William Perkin are true, according to the passage?*

A He taught Chemistry at a college in London.
B He believed that quinine could be artificially produced.
C He extracted the substance for his dye from a common plant.
D He quickly realised the financial benefits of his new creation.
E He set a new fashion trend for large skirts.

Questions 11–14

Complete the summary below.

Choose **NO MORE THAN TWO WORDS** *from the passage for each answer.*

The purple range of colours plays an essential role in colour therapy, a form of **11** .... Colour therapy is said to have originated many years ago in **12** .... and is still used by colour therapists such as Julia Kubler, who uses it to **13** .... with various health issues. According to Kubler, purple **14** .... aspects of two colours, making it both active and passive.

❸ Check your answers carefully. For Question pairs 7–8 and 9–10, make sure you have chosen TWO answers for each pair. For Questions 11–14, make sure that you have used no more than the maximum number of words allowed, your spelling is correct, and your answers make grammatical sense.

Listening Part 2

❶ You are going to hear the first part of a radio programme about a book on colour. Underline the key ideas around each gap in the table below and decide what information you need to listen for.

Questions 1–6

Complete the table below.

Write **ONE WORD** *for each answer.*

Spectrum by Alex Mackenzie

Title of chapter	Theme	Features
'The hidden jungle'	How an animal's colour and shape can conceal it when it hides or **1**	Has some outstanding **2** ....
'A question of choice'	Why people's colour **3** .... differ from others.	A **4** .... test which involves readers grading things based on colour.
'It's all in the **5** ....'	How our brain perceives colour.	Describes some **6** .... that the reader can do.

❷ Now listen to the first part of the Listening passage and complete questions 1–6.

❸ Read questions 7–10 below. Underline the key words or phrases in the <u>questions</u> and <u>options</u>.

Questions 7–10

Choose **TWO** *letters, A–E.*

Questions 7–8

According to the book, which of these **TWO** *effects are red and orange believed to have on shoppers?*

A They calm you down.
B They make you feel energetic.
C They give you an appetite.
D They make you feel enthusiastic.
E They encourage you to spend more.

Unit 2

Questions 9–10

Which of these TWO colours do people with a limited amount of money respond to the best?

A light blue   B purple
C orange   D pink
E red

4 🎧 Now listen to the next part of the Listening passage and answer questions 7–10.

Vocabulary
Phrasal verbs

1 Complete the passage with phrasal verbs from the box. You will need to change the form of some of the verbs. In one case, two options are possible.

bring up	carry out	come up with	end up
find out	go about	narrow down	point out
set up	start up	take up with	turn out
turn up	work out		

Janice loved art, was a keen painter, and dreamt of becoming a famous artist. However, since she was **1** ....*brought..up*..... in a house surrounded by lawyers (her father, mother and elder brother all worked for the family's legal business), it was generally expected that she would **2** .... doing the same thing when she finished university. Her father frequently **3** .... that working as a lawyer was one of the most satisfying jobs a person could have, and her mother **4** .... a special bank account where the money they gave her each birthday could be put aside to see her through university and law school. Meanwhile, family meals were **5** .... long discussions about the different types of law she should practise, with her parents finally **6** .... Janice's options to either corporate or family law.

Once at university, it didn't take her long to realise that law wasn't the profession for her, and after just one year at university she decided to leave education and **7** .... a gallery where she could sell her pictures. She asked her parents how she should **8** .... running a business like this, but disappointed with her choice, they refused to help. They just couldn't **9** .... why she had given up such a bright and promising future as a lawyer. Without their support, and without the right professional contacts, it was inevitable that her venture **10** .... to be a complete disaster, and she watched in dismay as all the money she had saved gradually disappeared.

However, she was an optimistic person, and knew that something would **11** ....
And one day it did. Through a friend, she **12** .... that a local advertising company was looking for an assistant in their corporate colour consultancy department. She applied for the job and was successful. Over the next few months, she **13** .... her duties diligently, displaying a degree of dedication and initiative that really impressed her employers. Consequently, when the company started looking for ways to attract more customers, Janice was one of the people they consulted. She was able to **14** .... lots of exciting and practical ideas, and as a result, customer numbers almost doubled within a few months.

Key vocabulary

2 Complete this passage with words from the box. In several cases, you will need to change the form of the word.

| except | house | hypothesis | improve | notice |
| purpose | scheme | set | strike | way |

It has been said that colour can influence people in such a **1** .... that it can alter their behaviour. This is an interesting **2** ....,
but how accurate is it? Recently, a prison in the USA **3** .... out to test it.

Colour my world

The prison, which 4 .... some of the most dangerous offenders in the country, had a bad reputation for violence among inmates. The cells and communal areas were painted a light green, which is supposed to have a calming effect. However, this particular prison proved to be an 5 ....: the colour clearly made little, if any difference to the way the inmates behaved. Changing the décor in the cells and communal areas (a colour 6 .... combining light grey and blue was chosen) failed to 7 .... this.

Then someone had an idea: why not change the colour of the prisoners' *uniforms*? After much debate, a 8 .... bright pink was chosen. The change was astonishing. Violence dropped 9 .... within just a few days, and within a few weeks had almost completely ceased to be a problem. To all intents and 10 ...., the colour had changed the prisoners' behaviour.

Grammar

Nouns and articles

❶ **Underline the correct answers (– = no article needed) in this extract from a newspaper article.**

'True Colours', **1 the / –** latest exhibition at **2 a / the** Museum of Art and Culture (MAC) in **3 the / –** Brockhampton city centre, is one of **4 a / –** series of events across **5 the / –** United Kingdom which is being funded by **6 a / the** Government Arts Council. It highlights **7 an / the** impact of **8 a / –** colour on our everyday lives, and provides **9 a / the** fascinating insight into many of **10 the / –** different ways colour is used to make **11 a / the** world brighter and more interesting.

MAC director Ted Markby explains why **12 a / –** colour was chosen as **13 the / –** theme of **14 the / –** exhibition. 'It's **15 a / –** remarkably powerful tool for all sorts of things,' he says. 'It creates or enhances **16 the / –** mood, it encourages or discourages you from doing certain things, and in many cases, when used in **17 an / the** advertising industry, for example, it can send **18 a / the** powerful message to **19 a / –** people. Can you imagine living in **20 a / the** world where it didn't exist?'

❷ **Now complete the next part of the article with *a*, *an*, *the* or –.**

To prove his point, he takes me into **1** .... first room, **2** .... mocked-up lounge where everything from **3** .... walls, floor and ceiling to **4** .... furniture and paintings is painted **5** .... dull shade of grey. 'It's lifeless and depressing isn't it?' he says. He then guides me into **6** .... next room, which is exactly **7** .... same, except that everything is painted in **8** .... bright, vibrant colours. **9** .... contrast between **10** .... two rooms is incredibly powerful, and for some inexplicable reason I suddenly start feeling hungry, even though I had **11** .... large breakfast just **12** .... couple of hours ago.

'That's quite **13** .... common response,' Markby says. 'Some visitors have even been known to ask **14** .... attendants if there's somewhere they can get **15** .... sandwich or bar of **16** .... chocolate. It happens because of **17** .... mental association between **18** .... food and colour that has been triggered by sudden exposure to all of **19** .... colours in this room. That's **20** .... sort of power it has!'

Writing   Task 2

❶ **Make a list of eight things you have bought recently. Then decide how important the <u>colour</u> of these things was when making your purchase: a) very important b) quite important c) not important at all.**

2 Read the following questions and complete the table.

1. Which of the places in the table below have you visited recently?
2. What was the predominant colour in these places?
3. How far do you think the predominant colours in these places influenced your decisions when it came to buying something: a) a lot b) some c) none at all?

Place		Predominant colour	Influence of colour
1	supermarket		
2	department store		
3	chemist		
4	sports shop		
5	electrical store		
6	book shop		
7	health food shop		
8	restaurant or coffee shop		

3 Read the Writing task below, then use your answers from Questions 1 and 2 above to help you decide whether the statement is (for you) either *mainly true* or *mainly not true*.

> *Colour is a powerful tool that is used to great effect by manufacturers and retail companies when they try to sell us something. In fact, many of the purchasing decisions we make are partly or largely influenced by colour.*
>
> *How true is this statement? How much does colour influence us when we buy something?*

4 Don't forget that in a discursive essay, you should provide one or two counter-arguments that go against your opinion.

For example:

Argument supporting your opinion:

When we go shopping for food such as fruit and vegetables, it is inevitable that we will choose food which looks ripe, and this is where colour is important. For example, we would rarely choose green tomatoes over red ones.

Counter-argument against your opinion:

Having said that, however, there are other factors that are equally important. These might include the size and shape of the fruit, the place it comes from, how it was grown, and of course the price.

Now plan your answer by writing some key notes in the table below.

- **Introduction:** My view – statement is mainly true / mainly not true
  ....

- **Second paragraph:** The colour of the things you bought and how important the colour was in making your choice.
  1 ....
  2 ....
  3 ....

- **Third paragraph:** The predominant colour in the places you visited and how those colours influenced your decisions.
  1 ....
  2 ....
  3 ....

- **Fourth paragraph:** Counter-argument(s) for any one or more of the above points.
  1 ....
  2 ....

- **Conclusion:**
  ....

5 Using your notes, write your answer in full. You should write at least 250 words, and spend about 35 minutes on the task. Make sure that your view on the subject is clear.

6 When you have finished, check your answer carefully. Make sure:

- you have answered the question properly. ☐
- you have expressed your attitude(s) clearly. ☐
- you have provided one or two counter-arguments. ☐
- your spelling, punctuation and grammar are correct. ☐

Colour my world

Unit 3 A healthy life

Listening   Part 3

❶ You are going to hear two people talking about some common painkillers (or *analgesics*). Before you listen, answer these questions:

1 When do people take painkillers (think of some specific examples)?
2 When would it not be good to take a painkiller?
3 Where can you get painkillers?

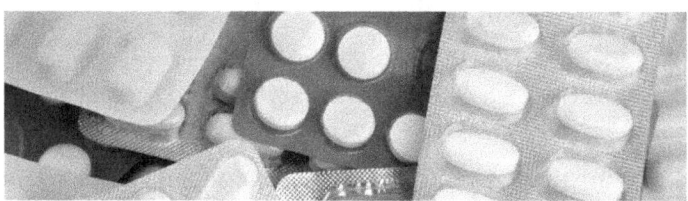

❷ Read Questions 1–5 in the Exam task below. Underline the key ideas in options A–F.

Questions 1–5

What comment do the speakers make about each painkiller?

*Choose **FIVE** answers from the box and write the correct letter, **A–F**, next to Questions 1–5.*

Common analgesics

1 Paracetamol ....
2 Ibuprofen   ....
3 Aspirin   ....
4 Codeine   ....
5 Morphine   ....

Comments

A It is considered unsuitable for children.
B It is extremely dangerous if you take too much.
C It is not as strong as other analgesics.
D Its use requires careful monitoring.
E It can have slightly unpleasant after effects.
F It works at the source of the pain.

❸ 🎧 Now listen to the first part of the conversation, and answer Questions 1–5.

❹ Look at Questions 6–10 below.

1 What does the flow chart show?
2 What type of word or words is needed to complete each gap?

Questions 6–10

Complete the flow chart below.

Write NO MORE THAN TWO WORDS for each answer.

Aspirin: a brief history

Ancient Greece, about 2500 BCE:
6 .... from willow trees are used to make a drink with a painkilling effect.

↓

Italy, 1823:
The 7 .... in the willow (salicin) is identified and extracted.

↓

Germany 1838:
Salicin is also discovered in the meadowsweet flower.

↓

France, 1853:
Salicin is first produced in a 8 .... (called salicylic acid).

↓

Germany 1893:
Acetyl is added to salicylic acid. Irritant qualities are reduced.

↓

Germany 1897:
A 9 .... of acetyl salicylic acid is first produced by Bayer (1897).

↓

Germany 1899:
Aspirin goes on sale in 1899 after successful 10 ....

❺ 🎧 Now listen to the second part of the conversation and answer Questions 6–10.

Vocabulary

Verb + noun collocations

1 **Use the words in the box to complete these extracts. The same word is missing twice from each one. You may need to change its form.**

| challenge | gauge | outline | overlook |
| promote | yield | | |

1 Many nutritionists are ...*challenging*... the assumption made by some that red meat is bad for you. In fact, they say, it has many positive health benefits. Naturally, those who say we should stop eating it altogether do not like to be .... this way, and are preparing a robust response.

2 It has long been known that taking regular exercise is an excellent way of .... a sense of well-being and all-round good health. Conversely, leading a sedentary lifestyle has the opposite effect. A new government advertisement is helping to .... awareness of the dangers of this.

3 A survey was conducted to .... people's attitudes to the government's proposed Medical Insurance bill. Most agreed that it will be difficult to .... the effectiveness of the bill until it has been put into practice.

4 The team .... one or two major points during the course of its research into the effects of the new drug. They didn't consider, for example, if there would there be side effects if taken with another drug. However, nobody could .... the fact that some of their findings would have important medical implications.

5 Recent research into the possible anti-cancer benefits of aspirin has only just begun to .... results. However, pharmaceutical companies who are investing heavily in the research programme are confident that their investment will .... excellent returns in the long run.

6 During the interview, the Health Secretary .... her strategy for improving the National Health Service. However, when the interviewer asked her to .... some of the ways these improvements might be paid for, she seemed unable to answer.

Key vocabulary

2 **Complete the passage by rearranging the letters in bold to make words and phrases. The first letter of each word is in its correct place.**

Last year, I became ill. At first, the
1 stompysm .... were not especially severe. I had frequent but
2 stroh-ldeiv .... headaches, my **3 jisnto** .... ached and I felt tired a lot of the time. Soon, however, my
4 ctiondion .... worsened. The headaches became more severe and I could hardly stay awake during the day. I started missing school, and because of my frequent
5 antesmbseei .... I started to
6 flal bniehd .... with my schoolwork. Unfortunately, my doctor couldn't diagnose what was wrong with me, and the painkilling
7 mcioedanti .... that he
8 pscedrreib .... failed to
9 reviele .... my aches and pains. Eventually he sent me to the hospital to
10 ugdnoer .... a series of tests. The doctors **11 evdatealu** .... the results, and then told me what they had discovered. It turned out that I had developed an intolerance to dairy products like cheese, and that was making me ill! They said that there was no way they could
12 ceru .... this intolerance, so now I can't eat dairy produce. However, I now feel a lot better.

A healthy life

Reading Section 3

❶ Quickly read the title and passage below, then choose an appropriate subheading (A–C) to go in the box after the title.

A Scientific research provides evidence that the more often children and old people exercise, the less likely they are to fall ill.
B Exercising for up to an hour a day can improve memory and learning for both young and old, scientists have found.
C Regular exercise benefits us all, whether young or old, but there are hidden dangers, scientists warn.

Scientific research reveals hidden benefits of regular exercise

Subheading:

Concerns that children in developed countries are leading increasingly sedentary lifestyles are growing. Recent research suggests that almost nine in ten children fail to get the 60 minutes of daily exercise which is the minimum recommended for good health, and a third completed less than an hour each week. In most cases, this is because they are spending hours every day glued to televisions, the Internet and games consoles. Alarmingly, there is evidence to suggest that this lack of exercise is not only having a negative physiological effect on them, but is also adversely affecting their academic performance at school.

Psychologist Dr Aric Sigman believes that regular exercise can significantly improve pupils' academic ability, and suggests that access to high-quality PE lessons is just as likely to have a long-term impact on children's education as time spent in conventional classrooms. He also supports the long-held conviction that vigorous physical activity is much better than moderate activity. 'Children should spend at least an hour a day doing some form of vigorous exercise,' he says. And his message to schools and parents is obvious. 'Schools and parents should devise ways of increasing physical activity in and out of school time.' This, he believes, is the key to improved academic performance.

For those who are sceptical about this, and no doubt there are many, he quotes two pieces of research that underline the link between physical activity and brain capacity. One study compared brain capacity and test scores among two groups of nine- and ten-year-olds, one with higher levels of physical fitness than the other. It revealed that fitter pupils had a twelve percent larger brain capacity than their peers, which was associated with better performance in cognitive tests. They were able to complete the test more quickly and got more answers correct. A second study of 1.2 million male teenagers in Sweden was perhaps even more revealing. It found that those who were fit were more likely to have a high IQ and go on to university.

Dr Sigman says, 'Physical activity is thought to help a child's cognitive processes by increasing blood and oxygen flow to the brain. This increases levels of chemicals like endorphin in the brain which decrease stress and improve mood. It also increases growth factors that help create new nerve cells and support the connections between brain cell synapses that are the basis of learning.

According to other researchers, there is also evidence that suggests regular exercise can increase the size of crucial parts of the brain, and that children who are fit also tend to be better at multi-tasking and performing difficult mental tasks than their unfit friends. Professor Art Kramer, director of the Beckman Institute for Advanced Science and Technology at the University of Illinois, who led the research, said their findings could have important implications for improving children's performance at school. He said it could also be used to help people combat memory loss and retain problem-solving skills in old age.

Unit 3

'It is a sad fact of ageing that our brain function decreases as we get older,' says Kramer. 'Increasingly, people are also living more sedentary lifestyles. While we know that exercise can have positive effects on cardiovascular disease and diabetes, we have found it can also bring about improvements in cognition and brain function. Aerobic exercise is best for this, so by starting off doing 15 minutes a day and working up to 45 minutes to an hour of continuous exercising, we can see some real improvements in cognition after six months to a year.'

Professor Kramer's team did a lot of neuroimaging work alongside their studies, which provided visual evidence to show that brain networks and structures actually change with exercise. This, they say, is the reason why their aerobically-fit test subjects were found to exhibit superior cognitive control to those who were less fit, and that regular exercise helped to improve memory, attention and an increased ability to multi-task. The hippocampus, that part of the brain involved in memory, of elderly people who exercised regularly for more than six months increased by two percent, effectively reversing brain ageing by one to two years.

Tests carried out on children also yielded some interesting results. One test involved them crossing a 'street' using a virtual reality simulation. Fitter children were better at crossing the street when distracted by music or holding a conversation on a hands-free mobile phone compared to those who were less fit. While both groups tended to walk at the same speed, the children who were less fit often misjudged the speed and distance of the computer-generated vehicles. 'The low fitness kids were just as good at crossing the street when it was the only thing they were doing,' says Kramer. 'If they were listening to music or talking on the headset, they performed badly. They often ended up with the screen going red to show they had been hit. One way to look at it is that fit children think more efficiently and so are better at multi-tasking.'

Professor Kramer presented his findings at the American Association for the Advancement of Science annual meeting in Vancouver, where other research presented showed that reducing the number of calories we consume could help to prevent brain disorders, especially in the elderly. Dr Mark Mattson, a neuroscientist from the National Institute of Ageing in Baltimore found that restricting people's diets to just 500 calories every other day increased production of proteins that are known to protect neurons from damage. 'There is considerable evidence that doing this is not only good for your heart, but is also good for your brain', he said.

❷ Read Questions 1–13, underlining key words and phrases, then find the answers in the passage.

Questions 1–5

Do the following statements agree with the claims of the writer?

Write

YES   *if the statement agrees with the claims of the writer*

NO   *if the statement contradicts the claims of the writer*

NOT GIVEN   *if it is impossible to say what the writer thinks about this*

1 The possible impact of a sedentary lifestyle on the way children perform in the classroom is very worrying. ....

2 It is only recently that people have discovered exercise is more beneficial for you when you put more effort into it. ....

3 It is unclear what Dr Aric Sigman thinks schools and parents should do. ....

4 There are probably a lot of people who disbelieve Dr Sigman's theory. ....

5 Researchers were surprised to discover a link between levels of fitness in Swedish teenagers and their IQ. ....

Questions 6–10

Complete the summary using the list of words, A–I, below.

Dr Sigman believes that when children do physical exercise, they experience less 6 .... as a result of a chemical change caused by increased blood and oxygen flow to the brain. Other researchers, such as Professor Art Kramer, think there is 7 .... that some parts of the brain become bigger, and fit children are better than unfit children at doing complicated 8 .... that require mental thought. Among other things, these scientific 9 .... could be used to benefit the 10 .... when it comes to fighting memory loss and keeping the skills that allow them to solve problems.

A ancients	D elderly	G performances
B anxiety	E exercises	H possibility
C discoveries	F anger	I proof

A healthy life ㉑

Questions 11–13

Choose the correct letter, A, B, C or D.

11 Which of the following is true, according to Professor Art Kramer?
  A People become less active as they grow older.
  B Exercising is an effective way of preventing diseases like diabetes.
  C One particular type of exercise is more effective than others.
  D When exercising, you should take short breaks during the exercise period.

12 What did Professor Kramer's neuroimaging work show?
  A Exercising physically alters the brain.
  B Unfit people have poor memories.
  C A particular part of the brain becomes more active during exercise.
  D Exercise can reduce ageing of the brain for up to two years.

13 What does *doing this* on line 110 refer to in the final paragraph?
  A changing the kinds of food we eat
  B eating no more than 500 calories a day
  C eating foods that are high in protein
  D eating less on certain days

Grammar

Expressing large and small differences

❶ **Complete the second sentence in each pair so that it has a similar meaning to the first sentence. Use the word in brackets, and one to four other words.**

1 There is more absenteeism in our London department than in our Birmingham department.
  (are)
  Absenteeism levels ......*are higher*...... in our London department than in our Birmingham department.

2 If you want to lose weight, eating smaller portions of food is not as effective as taking exercise.
  (less)
  If you want to lose weight, eating smaller portions of food is .... taking exercise.

3 There are fewer cases of heart-related illnesses since smoking was banned in public.
  (aren't)
  There .... cases of heart-related illnesses since smoking was banned in public.

4 These days I eat less red meat.
  (smaller)
  These days I eat .... red meat.

5 Improved health and safety regulations in the workplace have resulted in fewer accidents.
  (incidence)
  Improved health and safety regulations in the workplace have resulted in .... accidents.

6 These days, seeking medical treatment abroad is becoming more popular.
  (greater)
  These days, a .... people are travelling abroad for medical treatment.

7 Now that I'm revising for my exams, I have less time for exercise.
  (don't)
  Now that I'm revising for my exams, I .... time for exercise.

❷ **Each of the sentences above can be emphasised by the addition of one or two words. Insert the words into the sentences. In some cases, more than one answer may be possible.**

For example:

There is ↑ more absenteeism in our London department than in our Birmingham department.
far / much / a lot

Absenteeism levels in our London department are ↑ higher in our London department than in our Birmingham department.
far / much / a lot

Unit 3

Writing Task 1

❶ Look at the Writing task below. Read the question carefully, and highlight the key features in the chart and table.

The chart and table below give information about exercise and absenteeism in two departments of a major company.

Summarise the information by selecting and reporting the main features and make comparisons where relevant.

**Hours of exercise per week
(Figures based on 2012 survey)**

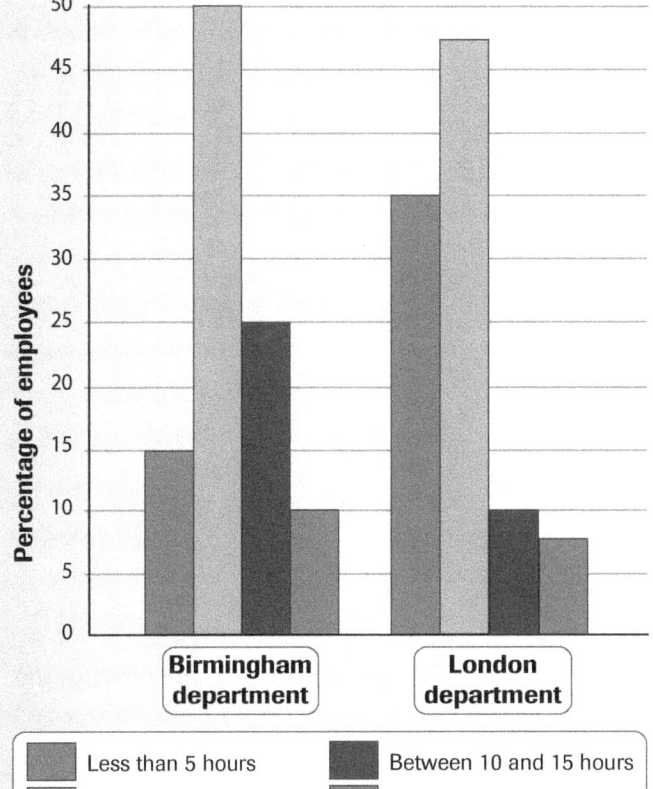

**Absenteeism through illness
(per 1,000 employees): 2012**

	Birmingham	London
No absenteeism	380	158
Between 1–5 days a year	378	594
More than 5 days a year	242	248

❷ Now choose the most appropriate introduction for a sample answer from A–C.

A The chart shows the number of people in two large companies who exercised on a regular basis over the course of a year, while the table shows how many of these people fell ill in the same year.

B The chart shows the amount of exercise taken each week by employees in two departments of a large company. The table shows the number of work days that were missed due to ill health during the course of a year.

C The chart shows the percentage of employees in a major company who exercised for between five and fifteen hours a week during a year. The table shows the results of this exercise on their attendance at work in the same year.

❸ Decide if these sentences are TRUE or FALSE based on the information in the chart and the table. If they are false, correct them.

1 In the chart, there are similarities and differences between the two departments. TRUE / FALSE
2 The percentage of employees in the Birmingham department who exercised for less than five hours was greater than it was in London. TRUE / FALSE
3 There was a big difference in the percentage of employees in both departments who exercised for between five and ten hours a week. TRUE / FALSE
4 A higher percentage of employees exercised for between ten and fifteen hours in London than in Birmingham. TRUE / FALSE
5 The percentage of employees exercising for more than fifteen hours was similar in both departments. TRUE / FALSE
6 In London, there were fewer employees who took time off work due to illness than there were in Birmingham. TRUE / FALSE
7 Most employees in the London department who took time off work did so for more than five days a year. TRUE / FALSE
8 The number of employees who missed more than five days of work was similar in both departments. TRUE / FALSE

❹ Now write an answer to the question. You should spend about 20 minutes on this task. Write at least 150 words. Remember to include an introduction (as Exercise 2 above), and don't forget to write a brief overview at the end.

Unit 4 — Art and the artist

Reading Section 1

1 Read the <u>title</u> and <u>subtitle</u> of the passage about photography and advertising below. How do you think the passage will be structured?

2 Quickly read the passage to check which period of history the writer covers.

Advert from the 1930s

A brief history of photography in advertising

Commercial photography has long had a significant place in the history of photography, and the advertising industry has been its largest benefactor.

In the late 19th century, photography was used only rarely to advertise products or businesses. Photographs occasionally appeared on business cards or as small informative pictures in catalogues and magazines, but it wasn't until the early 20th century that advertisers began to realise the enormous potential of this relatively new medium. At first, most preferred to use a 'reason why' strategy, with the result that their photographs just showed consumers the benefits of the product. However, when advertising psychologists in the early 20th century demonstrated that consumers were open to suggestion, they provided support for a new suggestive advertising strategy, often called 'atmosphere advertising'. Some more adventurous advertisers had already been experimenting with this, arguing that photographs did not need to show what a product could do, but could instead create a mood or feeling that people would associate with that product.

One of the inspirations for this strategy was American illustrator and photographer John Hiller who, in the early 1900s, was illustrating stories in women's magazines with photographs. He employed a soft focus technique, and used dramatic lighting and complex stage sets to create visually stunning pictures. His style was revolutionary for the time, and it gradually occurred to advertisers that this type of picture would be ideal for illustrating advertisements. As a result, photographs in advertisements suddenly became very popular. In 1920, fewer than 15 percent of illustrated advertisements in mass-circulated magazines employed photographs. By the end of the decade, this figure had soared to about 80 percent.

The tremendous new market for advertising photography provided a wealth of business opportunities for professional photographers. Clarence White, a successful pictorial photographer, led the way in training commercial photographers at his school in New York. He encouraged his students to apply a fine-art style of photography to industrial and commercial design, combining (as he put it) 'beauty and utility'. Some of his students went on to become New York's top commercial photographers. They practised a modernist style based on close-up views, spare geometric compositions, unusual vantage points and sharp focus that dominated advertising photography for the next twenty years. It was also at this time that images of real-life situations began to be used in advertising, a trend that became especially popular in the 1930s when the economic disaster of the Great Depression prompted advertisers to adopt the qualities of sincerity and realism in advertising imagery. The 1930s also saw technological progress in colour photography, and when commercial colour film went on sale for the first time in 1935, the widespread use of colour in advertising photography suddenly became much more affordable.

The dominant and most highly paid commercial photographer of the 1920s and 1930s was Edward Steichen. Like Clarence White, Steichen had been a pictorialist art photographer who turned to commerce. In 1923 he landed two commercial photography contracts – to produce fashion and celebrity portrait photographs for Condé Nast periodicals, and to produce advertising photographs for J. Walter Thompson, a major advertising agency. Over the next twenty years, he built up a huge client list, which included makers of beauty products, packaged foods, cars, jewellery and soaps. He was one of the first commercial photographers to work in close collaboration with his art directors, convincing them to look beyond conventional uses of photography in advertising (pictorialism for romance and suggestion; straight photography for information and reason-why). During his long career, he evolved a persuasive photography style that projected ideals, aspirations and obvious fantasies, but made them seem attainable.

By the 1940s, advertising was seriously big business, and vastly increased budgets meant that photographers working for the business could be more and more ambitious and experimental. The two best-known commercial photographers at this time were Irving Penn and Richard Avedon. While both continued to use photographic modernism in their advertising photography, they developed highly personal styles. Penn's pictures were characterised by a minimalist style which projected an image of calm elegance. Avedon's photographs were much more dynamic and conveyed an important message: the world was changing, and it was changing very quickly. His work, perhaps more than any other, was to influence future commercial photographers, and his style is still very popular today.

Commercial photography in the 1960s was less stylistically unified than in previous decades. It also saw a greater emphasis on internationalism and greater collaboration with art directors. Furthermore, there were huge changes in beliefs and attitudes, especially with regard to the way we behaved, or the way we saw ourselves and others. The advertising industry could not ignore this, with the result that newer representations of things like gender roles took their place alongside traditional ones. This set the tone for advertising photography in the remaining decades of the 20th century.

Advertising around the turn of the 21st century provoked new content-based controversies. Where mid-20th century advertising photography was often criticised for promoting overly traditional visions of life or unrealistic material aspirations, criticism of today's advertising has targeted images that glamorise unhealthy lifestyles. Criticism has also been directed at advertisements that appear to be trying to shock, offend or provoke rather than sell a product. One well-known clothing company, for example, received a lot of negative attention when it used powerful images of prisoners, refugees and a blood-covered T-shirt in a series of advertisements. These became notorious for their provocative content and led to a re-evaluation of what should and shouldn't be acceptable in advertising.

❸ Now answer Questions 1–13 below.

Questions 1–5

Complete the table below.

*Choose **NO MORE THAN THREE WORDS** from the passage for each answer.*

Significant moments in photographic advertising		
	Event	Reason or cause
1920s	Huge increase in number of illustrated advertisements using photographs.	Advertisers begin to realise that **1** .... photographs are perfect for advertising purposes.
1930s	Popularity of pictures showing **2** .... Colour in advertising photography becomes more widespread.	Advertisers respond to a serious financial crisis. **3** .... becomes available.
1940s	Commercial photographers become increasingly **4**	More money is available for advertising.
1960s	**5** .... are portrayed in a new way in advertisements.	Changes in beliefs and attitudes.

Art and the artist 25

Questions 6–9

Complete the flow chart below.

Choose **NO MORE THAN THREE WORDS** from the passage for each answer.

Edward Steichen

Turned to commercial photography after illustrating stories.

↓

In 1923, began taking pictures for magazines and a **6** ....

↓

Spent **7** .... working with many different companies.

↓

Persuaded art directors that they should be less **8** .... in the way they used photographs.

↓

Developed a **9** .... which made difficult or impossible things seem achievable.

Questions 10–13

Do the following statements agree with the information in the Reading passage?

Write

TRUE *if the statement agrees with the information*

FALSE *if the statement contradicts the information*

NOT GIVEN *if there is no information on this*

10 Advertising psychologists in the early 20th century came up with the idea for a new advertising strategy known as 'atmosphere advertising'. ....

11 John Hiller's photographs were often used to illustrate advertisements. ....

12 Photographs by Irving Penn and Richard Avedon contained both similarities and differences. ....

13 Some modern advertisers believe that people pay more attention to an advertisement if it contains deliberately provocative images. ....

❹ Check your answers. For Questions 1–9, make sure you have copied the words exactly from the passage, have used no more than the maximum allowed number of words, and check that your answers are grammatically correct in the context of the sentences.

Listening   Part 4

❶ You are going to hear a lecturer talking about ancient forms of art. Before you begin, look at these pictures and decide where they might originate from.

❷ Read through Questions 1–10 and decide:

1 which of the three art forms above you will hear being described, and the order in which they appear.
2 how the lecture is structured.
3 what type of information you need for each gap.

Unit 4

Questions 1–10

Complete the notes below.

*Write **NO MORE THAN TWO WORDS AND / OR A NUMBER** for each answer.*

Prehistoric visual art

Cave paintings

What are they?
Paintings in caves or on outdoor surfaces

How old?
Earliest paintings date back about **1** ....

Common themes
Animals, humans (and human hands), and
2 ....

Common materials
Ochre, manganese, oxide, hematite and other materials with **3** ....
Charcoal for outlines.

Best **4** .... paintings are those painted into cut silhouettes.

Possible purpose
Possibly believed to have **5** .... (to increase number of animals for food)

Petroglyphs

What are they?
Carved images in **6** ....

How old?
From 12,000 years ago until the 20th century

Common themes
Geometric designs, + humans / animals

Purpose
Possibly a kind of language.
Petroglyphs still possess great **7** ....

Interesting fact
Designs are universally similar (possibly due to the way the **8** .... is formed)

Geoglyphs

What are they?
Drawings or motifs on the ground.
Big: minimum diameter = **9** ....

Where found?
Worldwide.

Nazca Lines

Common themes
Creatures such as birds, monkeys, etc. (many **10** ....)

❸ 🎧 **Now listen to the lecture and complete the notes.**

❹ **Check your answers to make sure:**
- you have used no more than the number of words and / or numbers allowed. ☐
- you have provided a complete answer to each question. ☐
- your answer makes sense in the context of the sentence. ☐
- you have not made any spelling mistakes. ☐
- the word forms you use are the same as in the lecture. ☐

Vocabulary

Collocations and phrases with *make*, *take*, *do* and *have*

❶ **Complete these sentences with the correct form of *make*, *take*, *do* or *have*, and the words in the box.**

| account | advantage | ~~best~~ | business | choice |
| impact | mistakes | profit | research | use |

1 This painting is an excellent forgery. The artist has ......*done*...... his ......*best*...... to copy the original exactly, but if you look closely, you'll see that he has .... a few ....

2 As part of my dissertation on 20th century art, I've been .... some .... into the Pop Art movement and the .... it .... on the art world.

3 Many modern artists hate .... with art gallery owners because they feel that the owners are dishonest and .... of their lack of experience.

4 I recently sold some of my pictures at an art show, but after .... my expenses into ...., I didn't .... much of a ....

5 The Arts Centre at South Hill Park has two rooms that schools can .... of for lectures and talks. They .... a .... between the main hall, which seats 200, and a smaller lecture room for 50.

Key vocabulary

2 Underline the most appropriate word in bold in these sentences. In one case, either word is possible.

1 When it **comes / gets** to art, I have fairly broad tastes.
2 I like **visible / visual** art forms the most.
3 Good art should **grow / stimulate** the imagination more than anything else.
4 I admire anyone who can **make / produce** art, no matter how bizarre it is.
5 I particularly admire artists who can **create / exert** an influence on the art world.
6 For children, art is an ideal **vehicle / way** for expressing themselves.
7 The best way to **father / foster** artistic creativity in a child is to expose them to art from an early age.
8 Children should be given every **opportunity / probability** to develop their artistic talents.

Grammar

Expressing purpose, cause and effect

1 Complete this article with the words and phrases in the box. In one case, more than one answer is possible.

in order to	so that	on the other hand
for	whereas	as a result	otherwise
with the aim of	because	due to

Graffiti – Art or Vandalism?

Is graffiti art or vandalism? The majority of people see it as vandalism **1** .... they believe it is ugly, and reduces the value of private and public property. They also argue that **2** .... its illegal and anarchic nature, it attracts crime to an area. **3** ...., municipal authorities have to spend a significant amount of their annual budget cleaning up the mess that so-called 'graffiti artists' make, and installing expensive security cameras **4** .... deterring them.

Most graffiti consists of little more than scribbles, or 'tags', on a wall, typically put there at night **5** .... the perpetrator has less chance of being caught. Many question why they do it when there is a risk of capture and, invariably, a fine or even imprisonment. For some, the risk involved is the whole point, as they enjoy the element of danger. Others do it **6** .... fame and recognition, or they use graffiti as a means of self-expression. However, **7** .... many see graffiti as vandalism, others argue that those who paint walls are the avant garde artists of the early 21st century. One famous example is the man known only as Banksy, whose unique style of 'wall art', as it has become known, is instantly recognisable. Most graffiti artists hit and run at night. Banksy, **8** ...., sets up clever ruses to get his work on the walls. On one occasion, he even disguised himself as a city worker and closed a tunnel in London **9** .... redecorate its interior. He has also sneaked his work into some of the world's greatest art museums. Banksy's work now sells for a lot of money, and he counts many famous people among his customers. Those who frown on graffiti say that he is fortunate to have so many admirers, **10** .... he would just be another vandal.

Writing Task 2

❶ Read this Writing task. Brainstorm some reasons why you might agree or disagree with the statement. Also think of how you feel overall about it – do you <u>mainly agree</u> or <u>mainly disagree</u>?

> Write about the following topic.
>
> *It is pointless making children who lack artistic talent learn painting and drawing in Art classes at school. Instead, they should concentrate on other creative or practical subjects for which they may have more aptitude.*
>
> *To what extent to do you agree or disagree?*
>
> Give reasons for your answer and include any relevant examples from your own knowledge or experience.
>
> Write at least 250 words.

❷ Read this introductory paragraph from a sample answer written by someone who mostly disagrees with the statement, then order the sentences for the second and third paragraphs. The first sentence of each paragraph has been done for you.

In many secondary education systems around the world, there comes a point where pupils who lack talent in non-academic subjects like Art and Music are encouraged or made to switch subjects. It is generally believed that there is no point in making children do something that they have no aptitude for. In my view, this is the wrong approach.

Second paragraph

For a start, pupils who are taken out of Art classes will be making better use of their time at school.
= ....

Furthermore, by removing untalented pupils from Art classes, they will not be slowing other pupils down.
= ....

A second point is that trying, and failing, to do something you are not good at can be extremely demoralising, and this can have a powerful negative impact on a child's sense of self worth. = ...

Being held back by other pupils in a class can cause resentment and anger among those who are more capable. = ...

It is true that there are several convincing reasons in favour of the argument. = ...1....

Doing practical subjects like woodwork or IT skills, for example, will be much more useful to them later in life. = ...

Third paragraph

In fact, some of the world's greatest artists showed little artistic promise at school, but went on to produce paintings that now sell for millions of pounds. = ...

Above all, painting is pleasurable. = ...

However, I believe that there are more persuasive counter-arguments. = ...1....

Just because you are not good at something does not mean that you don't enjoy it, and learning should be fun as well as educational. = ...

For a start, children can develop a talent for art when they are given time and encouragement. = ...

Secondly, evidence suggests that creative activities like painting can improve overall academic performance and help children make sense of the world around them, even if they are not good at it. = ...

Children can also use art to express themselves. = ...

❸ Choose the best conclusion from the three below. Why would the other two not be appropriate?

1. In my view, all children should be encouraged to paint and draw. However, if it is clear that they lack talent, then it is something they should do in their own time, and Art classes at school should be left to those who show more artistic ability.
2. To summarise, children should not be made to do other subjects at school simply because they do not have as much artistic ability as others. Furthermore, many argue that learning to paint and draw at school helps children to temporarily focus their attention away from more academic subjects, and thus have time to process what they have learnt.
3. On the whole, I feel that all pupils benefit from learning to paint and draw, regardless of their artistic abilities. To deprive them of this opportunity could have negative consequences that may not be immediately obvious.

❹ Now write your own answer to the question in about 40 minutes, taking the view of someone who <u>mostly agrees</u> with the statement.

Art and the artist 29

Unit 5 Stepping back in time

Listening   Part 3

❶ Look at the picture and answer these questions.

1 What does an archaeologist do?
2 Can you think of any famous archaeological discoveries?
3 How can archaeologists tell how old something is?
4 What problems do you think archaeologists face?

❷ Before you listen, read through the questions and underline the key words.

Questions 1–5

Choose the correct letter, A, B or C.

1 What does Dave think about Professor Jeffcott?
A He's a typical archaeology lecturer.
B He's very enthusiastic about archaeology.
C He's not as interesting as some archaeology lecturers.

2 What was the first part of Professor Jeffcott's talk about?
A How it's now possible to date Neolithic structures more accurately.
B Artefacts that have been discovered on Neolithic sites.
C What Neolithic structures were used for.

3 According to Professor Jeffcott, most Neolithic structures …
A were built between two and three thousand years ago.
B were built by people before they moved from one place to another.
C were built during a period of change.

4 What fact about Neolithic people surprised the researchers?
A The kind of food they grew.
B The speed at which they developed new skills.
C The range of skills they had.

5 What is Dave going to do next?
A Study the way prehistoric buildings were built.
B Build a modern structure using prehistoric methods.
C Write an essay on prehistoric building methods.

❸ 🔊 Now listen to the first part of the conversation, and answer Questions 1–5.

❹ 🔊 Look at Questions 6–10, listen to the next part of the conversation, and complete the notes.

Questions 6–10

Complete the notes.

*Write **ONE WORD ONLY** for each answer.*

The Neolithic period: major events

9,000–8,000 years ago

6 ………………… of Neolithic people move around Europe.

8,000 years ago

England and France are 7 …………………

6,000–5,000 years ago

First 8 ………………… Neolithic housing appears.

About 4,500–3,000 years ago

Stonehenge built in 9 …………………

Pottery made and used for the first time.

Neolithic people start making 10 ………………… stone implements.

❺ Check your answers carefully.

Vocabulary

Word formation – negative affixes

❶ **Complete this passage with the correct form of the words in the box, adding prefixes or suffixes.**

| appear | direct | ~~estimate~~ | exist | hospitable |
| organise | practical | stable | worth | |

Extract from Memoirs of an Archaeological Dig

We arrived at the ruins in the middle of September, and immediately realised we had **1** _underestimated_ the problems we would be facing. For a start, the area was extremely **2** ....: daytime temperatures exceeded 50°C, there was little natural shade, fresh water was **3** ...., and the place was crawling with biting insects. What's more, as it was prone to frequent earthquakes, the whole area was very **4** .... To make matters worse, the clothes we had brought were totally **5** ...., offering little protection from the sun or against the mosquitoes which plagued the site. On the third day, our translator and guides **6** .... and we never saw them again.

At first, the excavation was extremely **7** ...., and after a week digging rather aimlessly in several hopeful-looking places, all we had found were a few **8** .... pieces of broken pottery. We decided that we had been **9** .... our energies, so instead decided to concentrate on a single spot by one of the temple walls. And that was when we made our discovery.

Key vocabulary

❷ **Complete each gap in this passage with between one and two words from the box.**

artefacts	heritage	implements	inheritance
insight	led	links	maintain	sentimental
value	widespread		

My most prized possession is a small, beautifully-preserved pottery horse that has been dated to the Iron Age. It's one of several ancient **1** .... that my grandfather found on his farm in the 1950s. Some of the other things he found included old farming **2** .... dating from the same period. Some of these provide a fascinating **3** .... into the way people used to farm the land. They were fairly **4** ...., so presumably the farm was built on the site of an Iron Age town or village.

My grandfather wasn't sure what the horse was for, but buried next to it was a broken pottery doll, which **5** .... him to believe it was a child's toy. It was part of my mother's **6** .... when my grandfather died a few years ago, and she passed it on to me. I don't think it's especially valuable, but it is of great **7** .... because it reminds me of my grandfather. I believe that things like this help us to **8** .... with our past, and while I know that the horse is part of our national **9** .... and belongs in a museum, I really can't bear to part with it!

Reading   Section 2

❶ **Look at the picture below and the title of the passage on page 32. What do you think the passage will mainly be about?.**

❷ **Now read the subheading for the passage. Were you right?**

❸ **Now read the whole passage and answer Questions 1–13 on page 33.**

Stepping back in time

When and why did we learn to stand on our own two feet?

We may never know for exactly how long humans have walked on two legs, and the debate about why we do it continues, but evidence and research give us plenty of clues.

A For many years, scientists and anthropologists disagreed about whether early humans started walking on two legs before or after their brain had increased. The predominant view was that brain size was important, and until our brains had reached a particular size and mass, bipedal movement would have been impossible. Then, in 1974, two scientists, Donald Johanson and Tom Gray, were mapping a remote area of Ethiopia when by chance they came across some fossilised bones which appeared to be from an early human, *Australopithecus afarensis*. Excavation of the site led to the discovery of several hundred more bones and bone fragments, all from a single skeleton. Scientific research of the bones later that year showed that they were 3.2 million years old and belonged to a young female hominid who the scientists nicknamed 'Lucy'. Most remarkably, however, the research showed that while Lucy had a very small brain compared with humans today, she was also bipedal.

B How did the scientists know this? Lucy's leg bones were angled relative to the condyles (knee joint surfaces), which allow bipeds to balance on one leg at a time when walking. There was also a prominent lip in the knee to prevent the patella (the knee cap) from dislocating due to this angle. Evidence was also found in Lucy's pelvis, which was able to accommodate an upright stance and the need to balance on only one limb with each stride. The shape of her ankle also showed that her big toes would have aligned with her other toes, which would have sacrificed manipulative abilities for efficiency in bipedal locomotion. Her feet, therefore, would have been used almost exclusively for getting around rather than for holding things. Finally, her backbone showed evidence of the spinal curvature necessitated by a permanent upright stance.

C Lucy's discovery was exciting for two reasons. Not only was she bipedal in spite of her brain size, but she was also believed to be our oldest ancestor. However, a discovery over thirty years later changed all that. In 2005, Professor Yohannes Haile-Selassie, head of Physical Anthropology at Cleveland Museum of Natural History, led an international team that discovered and analysed a 3.6-million-year-old fossilised partial male skeleton. It was found in the Woranso-Mille area of Ethiopia's Afar region, and it took Professor Haile-Selassie's team over five years to excavate. The team recovered the most complete clavicle and one of the most complete shoulder blades ever found in the human fossil record. A significant portion of the rib cage was also found.

D It was a significant find because this early hominid, also a member of *Australopithecus afarensis*, is 400,000 years older than Lucy, and significantly larger in size. Research on the new specimen revealed that advanced, human-like bipedalism occurred much earlier than previously thought. The specimen was nicknamed 'Kadanuumuu', which means 'big man' in the Afar language and reflects its large size. The male hominid stood between 1.5 and 1.7 metres tall, while Lucy stood only 1.1 metres tall. This individual was fully bipedal and had the ability to walk almost exactly like modern humans.

E Kadanuumuu's discovery was important for another reason. Despite all the research, there were still some in the scientific world who felt there was insufficient proof that Lucy walked fully upright. 'As a result of our discovery,' said Haile-Selassie, 'we can now confidently say that Lucy and her relatives were almost as proficient walking on two legs as we are, and that the elongation of our legs came earlier in our evolution than previously thought. Until now, all of our understanding of *Australopithecus afarensis*' locomotion has been dependent on Lucy. Unfortunately, because she was an exceptionally small female with very short legs, this gave some researchers the impression that she was not fully adapted to upright walking. This new skeleton falsifies that impression because if Lucy's frame had been as large as this specimen, her legs would also have been proportionally longer.'

F Professor Haile-Selassie's research goes a long way to explain *when* humans began walking upright. However, one tantalising question remains: *why* did we start walking upright? There are several schools of thought, but two are particularly compelling. One is that bipedal activity is linked to the need to carry as much as possible. 'Something as simple as carrying, an activity we engage in every day, might have, under the right conditions, led to upright walking,' says Dr Brian Richmond, who carried out research on bipedal movement in apes. 'Standing on two legs allowed early humans to carry more at one time because it freed their hands.' It is possible to observe this in apes. While many are capable of short bursts of bipedal movement, they only choose to do it when they need to carry something. And, interestingly, the more valuable the object is to them, the more they are prepared to walk on just two legs in order to carry it.

G However, another group of researchers working at the University of Arizona has conducted a study which suggests that walking upright is more beneficial because it saves energy. 'For decades now researchers have debated the role and evolution of bipedalism,' said David Raichlen, Assistant Professor of Anthropology. 'However, the big problem in the study of bipedalism was that there was little data out there.' Under his guidance, a group of researchers at the University trained five chimpanzees to walk on an exercise machine while wearing masks that allowed measurement of their oxygen consumption. The chimps were measured both while walking upright and while moving on their legs and knuckles. That measurement of the energy needed to move around was analysed alongside results from similar tests on humans. Raichlen discovered that humans walking on two legs use only one-quarter of the energy that chimpanzees use while knuckle-walking on four limbs. And of course using less energy means you need to eat less, which leaves more time for other things.

Questions 1–5

The Reading passage has seven paragraphs, **A–G**.

Which paragraph contains the following information?

1 The circumstances under which some animals walk upright. ....

2 An experiment to test a theory. ....

3 A lucky find which contributed to the debate about the way humans developed. ....

4 A new discovery compels scientists to reconsider how long humans have been walking on two legs. ....

5 The combined physical evidence which indicated the existence of bipedalism in early humans.
....

Questions 6–9

*Complete the sentences below. Choose **NO MORE THAN THREE WORDS** from the passage for each answer.*

6 Lucy was different from modern human beings because of, among other things, her ....

7 The positioning of her .... shows that Lucy would only have used her feet for walking.

8 It took scientists more than .... after Lucy's discovery to find a bipedal hominid that predated her.

9 The skeleton that Professor Haile-Selassie's team discovered was given its name because of ....

Questions 10–13

*Look at the following statements and the list of scientists, **A–D**, below. Match each statement with the correct researcher.*

10 The need to perform a basic function that we do on a regular basis may have resulted in bipedal movement. ....

11 It's much easier to carry heavy objects when you can move on two legs. ....

12 People have been talking about why humans walk on two legs for a long time. ....

13 We have further evidence that confirms something we already knew. ....

List of scientists
A Professor Yohannes Haile-Selassie
B Dr Brian Richmond
C David Raichlen
D None of the above

❹ **Check your answers carefully.**

Grammar

Using sequencers

❶ Complete this passage with words and phrases from the box. There is one word you do not need.

| as | as soon as | during that time | eventually |
| gradually | meanwhile | once | until | whilst |

I went abroad for the first time last year.
1 .... then, I had never been more than a few miles from my home. Quite by chance, **2** .... waiting for my flight at the airport, I met an old school friend. We hadn't seen each other for more than five years, and **3** .... he'd lost weight and grown a beard. However, I recognised him **4** .... I saw him. We went for a coffee, and **5** .... filled each other in on what we'd been doing since we had last seen each other. It was great catching up, but **6** .... my flight was called and we had to say goodbye. We swapped contact details, and agreed to meet up **7** .... we were back in the country. **8** .... , we promised to keep in touch by email.

Speaking hypothetically

❷ Underline the best words or phrases in *italics* in this passage. In some cases, more than one answer is possible.

In 1940, a group of teenagers discovered almost 2,000 beautifully-preserved rock paintings in a cave in Lascaux, France, when they were looking for their dog. These paintings **1** *may stay / may have stayed* a prehistoric secret **2** *had it not been / had not it been* for the wayward animal, which had gone exploring there. Once people started visiting the caves, however, the condition of the paintings began to deteriorate, so they were shut to the public in 1963. This was a good thing, as the paintings **3** *would probably be / would be probably* in very bad condition now **4** *had / if* the caves not been closed. These days, accredited scholars **5** *can / could* visit the caves, **6** *on condition that / provided that* they do not touch the paintings.

The Lascaux caves were not the only accidental archaeological discovery of the 20th century. In 1947, a young shepherd came across a selection of 2,000-year-old scrolls in a cave by the Dead Sea. These **7** *may not be / may not have been* found **8** *had it not / were it not* for a violent storm which caused him to take shelter there. The Dead Sea scrolls, as they are now known, consist of 8,000 biblical texts and have been able to tell historians a lot about the history of the region in that period. Everything, that is, except who the scrolls' authors were. **9** *If only we are / If only we were* able to travel back in time, they say, we **10** *could / should* find out who they were.

Writing Task 1

❶ Look at the diagrams in the Writing task. Match the captions, a–k, with the caption boxes 1–11.

(a) Water and water-borne chemicals between pebbles and grains ......9......
(b) Rocks and stones eroded to become pebbles and sand grains ....
(c) Expansion of cracks and fissures, and breaking of rock by frozen rainwater ....
(d) Sedimentary rock (sandstone or mudstone) eventually formed by the cementing of pebbles and grains ....
(e) Transportation of rock and stone fragments downstream ....
(f) Rock visible at low tide ....
(g) Rainwater in mountainside cracks and fissures ....
(h) River ....
(i) Layers of pebbles and sand grains on sea bed ....
(j) Dislodged rock and stone fragments ....
(k) Sea ....

Unit 5

The diagrams below show how sedimentary rock is formed in coastal areas.

Summarise the information by selecting and reporting the main features, and make comparisons where relevant.

Write at least 150 words.

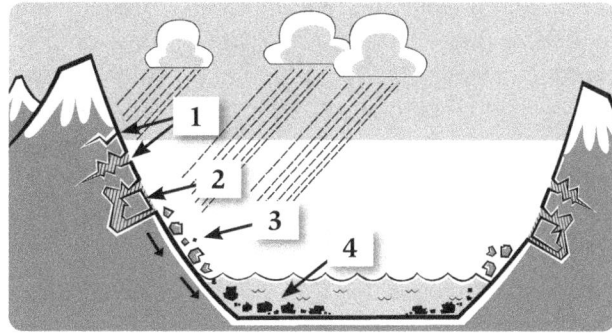
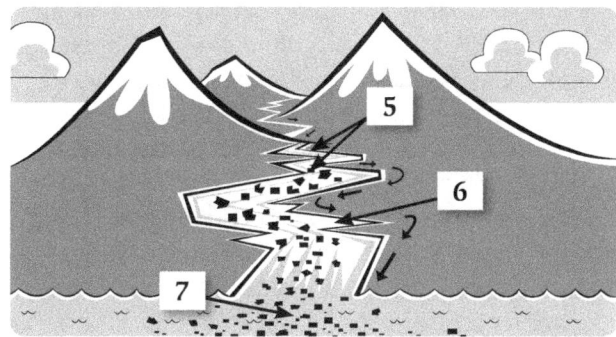
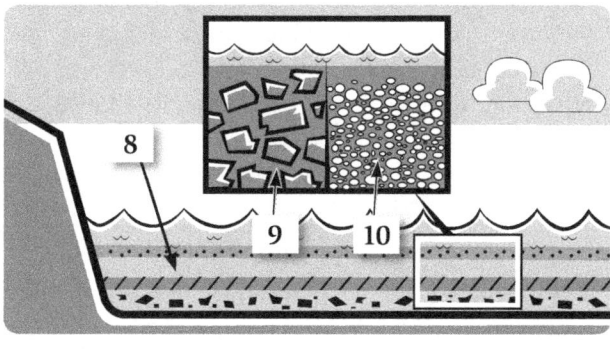
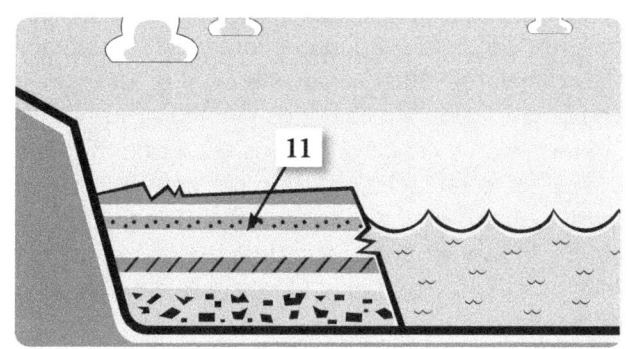

Coastal formation of sedimentary rock

❷ Look at these two introductions from a sample answer.

> A The diagrams show how rock and stone fragments are dislodged from mountains and carried to the sea. There the fragments eventually become sedimentary rock.

> B The diagrams show how rock and stone fragments are dislodged from mountains and carried to the sea, eventually .... sedimentary rock.

1 Complete introduction B using a different form of one of the words from introduction A so that it has a similar meaning.
2 Why is introduction B better than introduction A?

❸ These sentences also come from a sample answer. In each case, combine the two sentences by using a participle clause.

▶ Student's Book, page 121

1 The process begins when rain falls on the mountainside. It fills cracks and fissures with water.

   ....
   ....

2 The water freezes and expands the cracks and fissures. The rock around them is broken.

   ....
   ....

3 These sink in the sea. They form layers on the sea bed.

   ....
   ....

4 Water and water-borne chemicals work between the pebbles and grains of sand. They cement them together over time.

   ....
   ....

❹ Now answer the question, using the sentences in Exercises 2 and 3 and your own ideas. You should spend about 20 minutes on this task.

Stepping back in time

Unit 6 — IT society

Reading   Section 3

1 You are going to read a passage about a smart, green city called PlanIT Valley. First read it through quickly to get a general understanding, and then decide which of these subheadings is the best one.

- A Plans to build a smart green city in Portugal may be ambitious, but they are also surprisingly credible.
- B Ambitious plans for a smart green city in Portugal look good on paper, but it is doubtful they will ever be put into practice.
- C Innovative plans for a smart green city in Portugal could change the way cities of the future are built, but are they really worth it?

How Green is your PlanIT Valley?

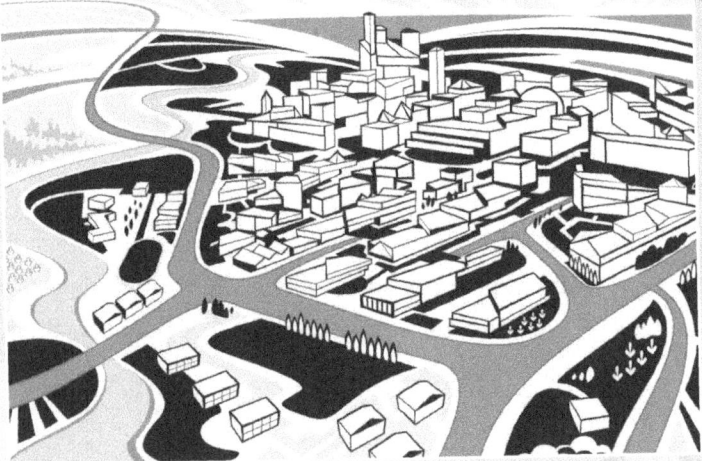

The first thing to say about the people running new European company Living PlanIT is that they are ambitious. Not only are they planning to build a smart green city from scratch at a site in northern Portugal, but they also hope to establish their PlanIT Valley development as both a genuine European alternative to the USA's Silicon Valley, and a working model that will inspire the next generation of low carbon cities. These will combine real environmental sustainability with a quality of IT-enhanced urban living almost unrecognisable from the crowded, polluted and disorganised reality that is city life for most people.

Many are sceptical about the company's plans for a brand-new smart city packed with cutting-edge green technology which can house 225,000 people while producing 'negligible' greenhouse gas emissions. To them, the technical challenges, combined with the $10 billion that the company needs to raise to see the project through from beginning to end, make Living PlanIT's plans sound more like an admirable experiment rather than a viable construction project. Their scepticism is not helped by the company's use of marketing language that, in order to understand it, requires a degree in Public Relations. For example, the company's claim that its 'design and manufacturing platforms enable the convergence of computing, network and sensing technologies with the fabric of buildings and places, demonstrated at urban scale in the development and operations of PlanIT Valley' does not really explain what it does.

However, when you listen to chief executive Steve Lewis outline his plans for the company, it becomes possible to believe that they might just deliver on their absurdly ambitious promises. His rationale for the company is admirably simple. He argues that the construction industry remains the last sector of the economy to resist the IT revolution that has enhanced efficiencies across every other industry, from car manufacturing to food production. Their existing techniques are inadequate, he says, for today's technology-rich and environmentally-aware requirements. Here, therefore, is an opportunity to entirely update the building process. Taking lessons from other manufacturing industries, including aerospace, automotive and shipbuilding, project leaders identified a number of elements that feature in modern manufacturing processes and which could be applied to modern buildings from the very start of the construction process.

Living PlanIT plans to integrate IT into the fabric of the city. It is installing many thousands of sensors that allow an urban operating system to deliver intelligent buildings that are constantly optimised to enhance comfort, productivity and environmental sustainability. Meanwhile, the latest renewable energy technologies and green building techniques will allow the city to operate with a virtually non-existent carbon footprint. Of course, such techniques are not new, but they are rarely put into practice. In fact, the IT industry has been complaining for a long time that the construction sector has failed to make adequate (if any) use of IT in its buildings.

line 39

So, what makes PlanIT Valley different? For a start, the company has considerable power and influence, both in terms of the team it has assembled and the financial backing it has already been promised. Lewis and many on the senior management team have served as senior executives with other major IT companies. This means that they not only have the right experience, but also the essential 'anything is possible' mentality that is a feature of such companies. In addition, Lewis claims that the company has already invested $300 million in putting together its team of engineers and developing its technology portfolio. As a result, the project is establishing a degree of credibility that far exceeds that of other similar projects.

More importantly, however, almost all of the technology the company is planning to deploy in PlanIT Valley either already exists or is viable from a technical point of view. Intelligent buildings that know to turn the air-conditioning on before you even realise you are hot may sound like something out of a science-fiction novel, but we are increasingly living in a science-fiction age. You do not need to invent anything new to develop a zero-carbon smart city, you just have to put all the right technologies together in the right place.

If Living PlanIT achieve this integration, it will hopefully be able to prove the final part of Lewis' claim. Namely, that cost concerns surrounding green developments are ill-founded. A more automated approach to construction coupled with long-term efficiency gains delivered by intelligent infrastructure more than cancel out the extra money required to build the development in the first place. And if it can win the economic argument, future opportunities are enormous. As Lewis points out, projected world population growth means that the world has to deliver between 9,500 and 10,000 new cities over the next forty years to house everyone. There is no chance of avoiding dangerous levels of climate change unless this expansion is delivered in an environmentally-sustainable manner. That would provide quite a business opportunity for the company that can deliver the solution.

The PlanIT Valley project presents many problems in terms of project management and coordination, and there is a huge amount of work to be done before the first residents are able to move in. Whatever the outcome, it is hard not to admire a project that will put so many theories about smart cities to the test all in one go. First, it is challenging accepted assumptions on how cities should be designed and constructed. Secondly, it will show what can be done if connectivity and intelligence are built into the design from the beginning. Thirdly, it will be a pilot project for a whole range of new services and, equally important, new types of collaboration.

❷ Now answer Questions 1–14 below. Remember to underline key words and phrases in the questions and options A, B, C and D first.

Questions 1–5

*Choose the correct letter, **A**, **B**, **C** or **D**.*

1 What do we learn about the people running the company Living PlanIT in the first paragraph?
   A They are going to build the world's first green smart city.
   B They want to build a replica of Silicon Valley in Europe.
   C They want their new city to be the first of other similar cities.
   D They think that the quality of life in most other cities is unacceptable.

2 Why are a lot of people sceptical about PlanIT Valley?
   A They do not think that the plans are practical or possible.
   B They do not understand how the technology works.
   C They have misunderstood the reasons why Living PlanIT is building a new city.
   D They have not read the marketing information clearly enough.

3 Who or what does *Their* in *Their existing techniques* refer to in line 39?
   A Living PlanIT
   B The construction industry
   C Car manufacturers
   D Food producers

4 The senior management team at Living PlanIT
   A have more power and influence than teams working on other, similar projects.
   B have raised enough money to build PlanIT Valley.
   C work elsewhere when they are not working on the PlanIT Valley project.
   D possess the right attitude required to undertake such a major project.

5 Why, according to the author, is the PlanIT Valley project so admirable?
   A It shows how good working practices can have a successful outcome.
   B It presents such a challenge to its creators.
   C It is putting several theories into practice simultaneously.
   D It demonstrates why collaboration between builders and IT experts is so important.

Questions 6–10

Do the following statements agree with the claims of the writer in the Reading passage?

Write

YES   *if the statement agrees with the claims of the writer*

NO   *if the statement contradicts the claims of the writer*

NOT GIVEN   *if it is impossible to say what the writer thinks about this*

6 Living PlanIT's marketing information is unclear and confusing for many people. ....

7 Steve Lewis presents a convincing argument that suggests PlanIT Valley might succeed. ....

8 Some of the buildings in PlanIT Valley have features that can be found in aircraft, cars or ships. ....

9 Living PlanIT's idea of building a smart, environmentally-friendly city is original and unique. ....

10 Some of the technology in PlanIT Valley was probably inspired by science fiction stories. ....

Questions 11–14

Complete each sentence with the correct ending, **A–G**, below.

11 The IT industry believes that, when it comes to putting up new buildings, IT is currently ....

12 Creating new technology for PlanIT Valley is ....

13 Steve Lewis believes that the economic arguments against green developments are ....

14 Some organisational aspects of the PlanIT Valley project are ....

A	technically possible	E	inefficient
B	underused	F	too ambitious
C	difficult to avoid	G	extremely challenging
D	not valid		

Listening   Part 4

❶ **You are going to hear part of a lecture about internet banking. What advantages and disadvantages are there in using a computer to access your bank account?**

Advantages	Disadvantages

❷ **Look at Questions 1–12 below. Decide what kind of information you need for each gap, and what type of word or words. Pay particular attention to the words immediately preceding and / or following each gap, as these will sometimes give you a clue as to the type of word.**

❸ 🔊 **Now listen to the lecture and answer Questions 1–12.**

Questions 1–12

Complete the notes below.

Write **NO MORE THAN TWO WORDS AND / OR A NUMBER** *for each answer.*

Internet banking

History

<u>1980s</u>

- Early online banking access required a computer, a monitor and a **1** ....
- Very basic. Customers could only:
  - see their **2** ....
  - send messages to their bank.

- 3 .... were required to move money to other accounts or make bill payments.
- Under one percent of bank customers made use of early online banking.

1990s

- Sharp rise in number of 4 .... following establishment of Internet.
- Modern online-banking services using web browsers begin.
- Initial consumer reluctance to carry out financial transactions online (5 .... from accounts often occurred).
- Changing consumer attitudes prompted by:
  - better 6 .... on banking websites
  - more online stores (e.g., Amazon, eBay).

2000+

- 2001: Bank of America = first bank with three million online customers (making three million payments to a value in excess of one 7 ....).
- 2012: As many as 8 .... of bank customers banking online in one country.
- Many online (internet-only) banks open.

Benefits of internet banking

Customers:

- They have access to accounts 24/7
- They can make payments (gas, electricity, etc.), move money between accounts, 9 ...., etc. No need to go to bank.
- They can access banking services using computers or 10 ....

Banks:

- Customers keep more money in their account.
- Reduced need for customer 11 .... staff.
- Increased customer loyalty (+ more recommendations to others).
- Lower running costs (internet banks only).
- 12 .... banks can find customers elsewhere (+ therefore operate beyond their usual area).

Vocabulary

Adjective + noun collocations

1 Complete this film review with words from the box. In some cases, more than one answer is possible.

achievements	characters	considerable
expectations	features	high	main
noteworthy	number	outstanding

Super Creepies (Bananaflix Studies. On general release 16 April. Certificate PG)

CGI animation has come a long way in the last fifteen years, with Bananaflix Studio's 2012 *Birdies* being one of the animated film industry's most 1 *outstanding achievements*, winning multiple awards and making over £100 million at the box office. It is only natural, therefore, that cinemagoers will have 2 .... for their latest offering, *Super Creepies*. Ultimately, however, I suspect they will be disappointed. This film is wrong at several levels. From a production point of view, the animation is clunky and there are a 3 .... of very obvious continuity errors. In addition, the storyline is weak, the dialogue is dreadful, and it is very hard to relate to the 4 ...., who are for the most part rather unlikeable (and, in some cases, quite scary, especially for younger viewers). A couple of amusing songs do little to enhance the film's appeal, and despite a couple of 5 .... (the vivid, vibrant colours, for example, practically leap from the screen), *Super Creepies* will fail to find many fans. Poor★★

Key vocabulary

2 Complete the sentences with a preposition or particle to form an expression with the word(s) in bold.

1. The way we communicate was radically altered by **the advent** .... the Internet.
2. Social network sites mostly seem to **cater** .... young people.
3. Internet technology has advanced .... **leaps and bounds** in the last few years.
4. The trouble with some social networking sites is that once you're **engaged** .... conversation with fellow users, it's hard to stop!

5 Last night's documentary on internet gaming was interesting, but it **glossed** .... the main points.

6 .... **essence**, the message is very simple: if you don't want to be a victim of internet crime, don't shop online!

7 I find it difficult not only to talk to, but also to **identify** ...., people who spend all their time glued to their mobile phones.

8 If you want to contact the company, open their website, **scroll** .... the page until you see 'Contact us' near the bottom, and click on it.

9 My attempts to fix my computer were all .... **vain**, and eventually I had to take it to a computer repair shop to sort it out.

Grammar

Referencing

Complete this passage with words from the box. You will need some of the words more than once. There are three words you do not need.

| it | me | that | them | us | these |
| their | him | they | this | those | her |

My new car has an on-board computer which controls a variety of features designed to make driving both safer and easier. One of **1** .... is something called a *pre-safe system*. **2** .... performs a simple but vital function – to anticipate a crash and prepare the car to keep **3** .... and my passengers safe.

So how does the system work? Sensors at the front of the car continually monitor the vehicles ahead. If **4** .... suddenly stop or slow down, the sensors send a warning to the on-board computer. **5** .... then does three things. First of all, **6** .... sets off an alarm to warn **7** .... that there are slow or stationary vehicles ahead and I need to take action to avoid **8** .... **9** .... then primes the brakes, so that by just slightly touching the brake pedal, I will apply **10** .... full force to the wheels. Finally, **11** .... reduces engine power, slowing the vehicle down to prevent it from hitting **12** .... which have stopped or slowed down ahead. If the computer sees that a

crash is unavoidable, **13** .... tightens the seatbelts and prepares to deploy the airbags. All of **14** .... happens in less than a second.

More and more cars are having **15** .... systems installed to protect **16** .... occupants in the event of an accident. No doubt **17** .... will save many lives. Having said **18** ...., however, I do wonder if people might become more careless drivers as a result.

Writing   Task 2

❶ **Look at this Writing task. Underline the key ideas.**

> *Over-reliance on modern technology means that people are failing to learn, or are forgetting, many basic skills.*
>
> *To what extent is this true? Are people becoming so reliant on modern technology that they are no longer able to do some things without it?*
>
> *Give reasons for your answer and include any relevant examples from your own knowledge or experience.*
>
> *Write at least 250 words.*

❷ **Think of some skills that people are failing to learn or forgetting because they rely too much on modern technology. What are the possible consequences? For example:**

Item of technology	Satellite navigation (sat nav)
Skill lost	How to read maps
Consequence	People end up in strange places because sat nav is not always accurate.

Unit 6

3 Here is the introduction and the beginning of the second paragraph from a sample answer. Complete each gap with one word from the left-hand box and one from the right-hand box.

biggest	detrimental		benefits	drawbacks
huge	integral		effect	part
invaluable			resource	

Modern technology has become an **1** .... of our everyday lives, and has brought **2** .... In many cases it has made certain tasks much easier. However, technology designed to simplify things can have a **3** .... One of the **4** .... is that people have become so reliant on it that they are not acquiring some basic life skills.

Take satellite navigation (sat nav) systems, for example. Although they are an **5** .... for people such as taxi and lorry drivers, many people are no longer learning how to read a map.

4 The writer uses two discourse markers above to make a counter argument. Identify them, then use them to complete these sentences.

1 Technology has many advantages, ... we need to make sure we use it responsibly.
2 Technology has many advantages. ...., we need to make sure we use it responsibly.
3 .... technology has many advantages, we need to make sure we use it responsibly.

5 Use these other discourse markers to complete sentences 1–6. In some cases, more than one answer is possible.

| even though | in spite of this | nevertheless |
| on the other hand | whereas | while |

1 Some photo processing software is very easy to use, ... some takes months to master.
2 My new computer keeps crashing, ... it's supposed to be one of the most reliable ones available.
3 My old mobile had lots of useful apps. My new one, ..., has lots that I don't think I'll ever use.
4 The word processing programme on my computer has a spell check feature. ...., my last essay was full of spelling mistakes.
5 .... I'm keen on modern technology, I sometimes feel we rely on it too much.
6 I don't like tablet computers. ...., I can see why a lot of people do.

6 Can you think of one or two advantages for each of the items or applications you mentioned in Exercise 2?

Item or application	Advantages
Satellite navigation system (sat nav)	- helps prevent traffic congestion - reduces traffic accidents

7 Now write your own answer to the Writing task. You should spend about 40 minutes on this task. Use your own ideas, try to provide at least two or three counter arguments, and use discourse markers where relevant.

IT Society

Unit 7 Our relationship with nature

Listening Part 3

1 You are going to hear a student asking his tutor for some advice about bird watching. Before you listen, consider the following:

1 Have you ever been bird watching, or have you been somewhere to observe other animals in the wild?
2 Why do people observe animals in the wild?
3 What advice do you think the tutor will give the student? Try to think of five or six things.

2 Read through Questions 1–10 below. Are there any answers that you might be able to predict before you listen?

3 🎧 Now listen to the first part and answer Questions 1–5.

Questions 1–5

Complete the sentences.

*Write **NO MORE THAN TWO WORDS** for each answer.*

1 Choose binoculars that are comfortable to carry and have excellent ....
2 Follow the birds the way a .... would follow them.
3 .... if you can, so the birds don't see you.
4 Listen to the noises the bird makes, and observe what it looks like (its ...., shape, markings and other characteristics).
5 Observe movement and flight patterns, ... and habitat.

4 🎧 Now listen to the rest of the conversation and answer Questions 6–10.

Questions 6–8

Label the plan below.

*Write the correct letter, **A–G**, next to questions 6–8.*

6 Goose hide ....
7 Eagle hide ....
8 Cuckoo hide ....

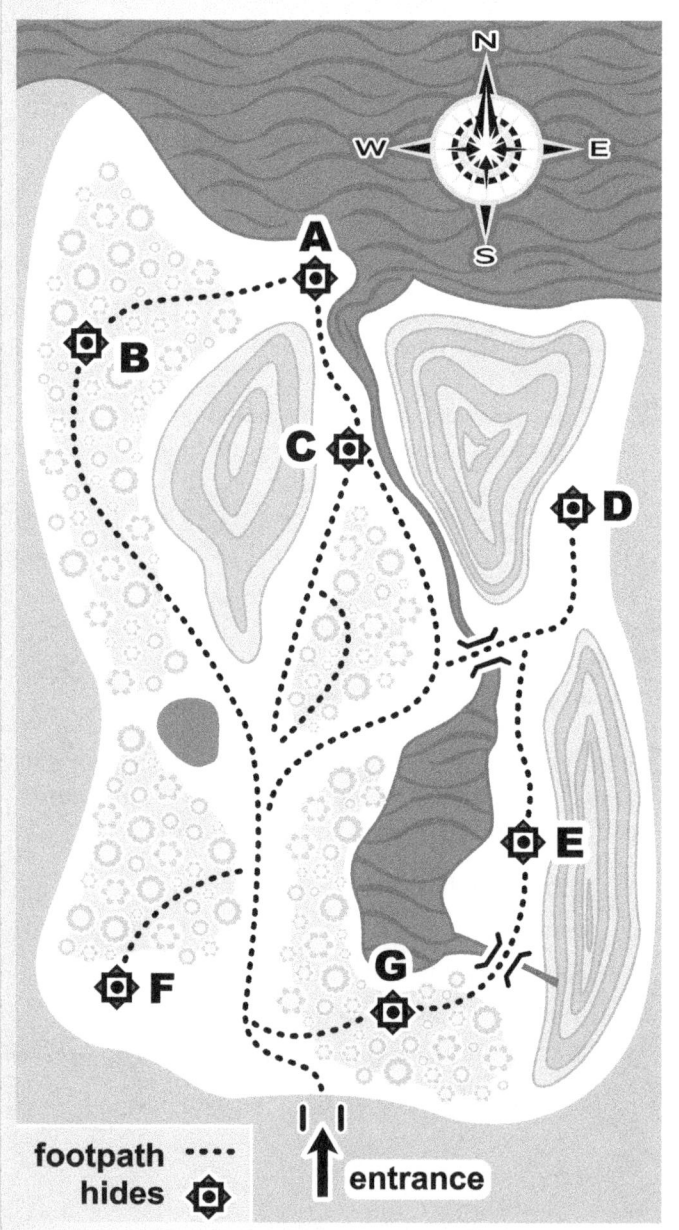

Questions 9–10

Answer the questions.

Write ONE WORD ONLY for each answer.

9 What, according to the tutor, helps to make bird-watching especially enjoyable? ....

10 Apart from binoculars, what should the student take with him? ....

5 When you have finished, check your answers carefully.

Where relevant:

- have you used no more than the allowed number of words? ☐
- do your answers make grammatical sense? ☐
- is your spelling correct? ☐
- have you only used the words you hear in the conversation? ☐

Vocabulary

Idiomatic expressions

1 Complete the passage with words and expressions from the box to make idiomatic expressions. In some cases, more than one answer is possible, and you will need to use one word twice.

bear	in mind	in the	into account	long run
make	put it down	take	the most of	
to experience	your breath away			

Bird-watching is a very enjoyable pastime, but there are one or two things you should **1** .... **2** .... before you head off to the nearest wood with your binoculars. First of all, you need to **3** .... the time of day **4** .... Birds are at their liveliest early in the morning, so to **5** .... **6** .... your bird-watching experience, you'll need an early start. Secondly, although you'll occasionally see a magnificent bird that will **7** .... **8** ...., such as an eagle or hawk, you'll mostly be watching common birds like sparrows, robins or blackbirds. In fact, there will be occasions when those are all you see. Don't give up, however. Be patient, and **9** .... **10** .... you'll be rewarded with the sight of an eagle soaring majestically over the hills or a hawk diving on its prey. And if that doesn't happen, **11** .... **12** ...., pack up your binoculars and head to the nearest zoo. You'll find hundreds of birds there, and you can study them at leisure for as long as you like!

Key vocabulary

2 Complete sentences 1–9 with verbs and adjectives from the box, then use the letters in bold (in the same order they appear in the sentences) to make a word to complete sentence 10.

| bo**l**ster | **c**loning | for**a**ge | num**e**rous |
| st**u**nning | temp**t** | thr**i**ve | **t**oxic | **v**iral |

1 .... a plant or an animal means you create a copy of it which has exactly the same genes.

2 A very good view is often described as ....

3 You can .... someone's confidence, the economy or your own image.

4 You can .... someone to do something by offering them some sort of payment or reward.

5 A plant, person, business or economy will .... under the right conditions.

6 A .... infection is an infection caused by an extremely small organism.

7 When you .... for food, you go from place to place searching for it.

8 Industrial waste and chemicals are often ....

9 There are .... ways of encouraging wildlife to urban areas, planting trees being just one of them.

10 You can .... crops, a relationship or an image of yourself.

Our relationship with nature

Reading   Section 2

❶ **Quickly read through the passage below, and complete this sentence:**

The passage is mainly about …

A the effect humans are having on various ecosystems.
B different ways in which certain species can be identified.
C the way living organisms all affect one another in some way.
D research into the way endangered species can be saved.
E opposing views about why some species are becoming extinct.

❷ **Number these things in the order in which they are mentioned.**

A

B

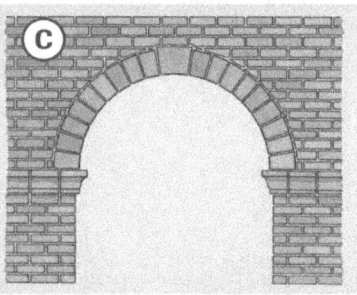
C

D

E

F

G

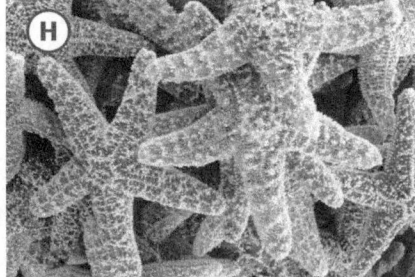
H

Keystone species

Some species are crucial when it comes to maintaining a well-balanced ecosystem.

A In the world of wildlife conservation, it is usually animals like whales and tigers which get the most public attention. Consequently, projects to protect these so-called 'flagship species' receive the greatest amount of funding, and this helps to ensure, or at least improve the chances of, their long-term survival. However, it could be argued that perhaps we should be focusing more attention elsewhere. This is because many of the minute plants, insects and microorganisms that we tend to ignore actually play a far more important role in biodiversity protection. Consider, for example, the Western honeybee *Apis mellifera*. Regarded as one of the world's most efficient pollinators, the honeybee plays a direct or indirect part in the production of many food products in our markets and stores. However, in recent years, a problem known as 'colony collapse disorder' has manifested itself, and now honeybee colonies are rapidly disappearing. Nobody knows the cause of this phenomenon, but the implications are worryingly clear: unless a solution to colony collapse disorder is found soon, food production will be seriously, perhaps disastrously, affected.

B The honeybee example illustrates how everything in the natural world is connected, and how the disappearance of one species can have a profound effect on the ecosystem around it. To understand how this happens, imagine an arched doorway or window in an ancient stone building. Many buildings containing arches are still standing today, hundreds, or even thousands, of years after they were built, in spite of the ravages of time and natural disasters such as earthquakes and floods. If you examine one of the arches carefully, you will see the reason why. On each side of the arch, there is a vertical series of bricks which gradually curve inwards, and these are supported at the centre by a keystone. It is this keystone that gives the arch, and the structure around it, its strength and stability. Once the keystone is put in position, the arch can stand indefinitely. Remove it, however, and the whole thing collapses.

C In the same way that an archway relies on its keystone to stay standing, so the ecosystem in a particular area relies on certain species in order to continue functioning. Named 'keystone species' by zoologist Robert Paine, who undertook the first major study of the effect of species loss on local environments, they have a major influence on the ecosystem around them. And there are a surprisingly large variety of them. Some are carnivores and some are herbivores. Some are marine and some are terrestrial. Some, like the huge, majestic African elephant, dominate their landscape, while others, like tiny microorganisms, are invisible to the human eye.

D At first glance, it is hard to imagine how the disappearance of one of these species could have such an effect on its environment. However, as Paine discovered when he carried out a series of experiments in the 1960s, the impact can be extreme. The subject of his first study was the starfish *Pisaster ochraceous*. When Paine removed a large number of these fish from part of Mukkaw Bay in the USA, he observed sudden changes in species diversity. The mussel and sea urchin population increased, since these creatures form an important part of *Pisaster's* diet. However, other species saw a dramatic decline. Paine counted fifteen species at the beginning of his experiment, but only eight remained at the end. Furthermore, reefs in the area were also destroyed, as increasing numbers of sea urchins fed on their coral. In another area of the bay, where the starfish community was left undisturbed, no changes were observed. Paine also observed that once *Pisaster* was returned to the area he had removed it from, the ecosystem began a gradual return to its pre-experiment state. His experiment prompted ecologists and conservation biologists around the world to identify other keystone species using similar removal experiments to find them. Over the next thirty years, the list of keystone species increased rapidly.

E Unfortunately, significant changes in other interconnected populations are taking place without removal experiments being carried out, with some keystone species being driven close to extinction. For the last ten years, Professor David Gomm of the Marine Conservation Association has led a study of sea otters in the North Pacific. This keystone predator feeds on sea urchins, which in turn feed on the vast kelp forests in the region. 'At the beginning of our study, sea otters were very common in the area, and so the kelp forests were thick and healthy,' says Professor Gomm. 'However, for a number of reasons, killer whales have begun to include otters in their diet, and this has caused sea otter populations to fall rapidly. Consequently, sea urchin populations have exploded, and this has led to an almost total destruction of the kelp forests.' He believes that if sea otters become extinct, other species will follow. 'The ecosystem would be changed forever,' he warns.

F Professor Gomm's prediction may sound overly dramatic to environmental sceptics, but there is an indication that it might already have happened. The species in question is, or rather was, the dodo, a large, flightless bird that once lived on the island of Mauritius. In the late sixteenth century, the bird's population began to fall sharply as European settlers arriving on the island cut down the forest where they lived and introduced dogs, cats and rats, which raided their nests for their eggs. By the end of the seventeenth century, the dodo was extinct. Today, it is often regarded as little more than a rather slow-witted bird that was unable to adapt. However, there are some who believe it may have been a keystone species. For evidence of this, they point to a tree called the tambalacoque. Once common across Mauritius, there are now only a few dozen left at most. It is thought that the dodo ate the fruit of the tambalacoque and activated the seed through unique digestive processes. With the demise of the dodo, tambalacoque numbers declined to just a few trees, reducing a valuable food source for other animals on the island.

G Some scientists are doubtful about the connection between the dodo and the tambalacoque. After all, they argue, if the tree was dependent on the dodo, why are there still some growing on the island? However, they all agree that even if there is no direct connection, the study does help to make an important point: even though a species may seem unimportant in isolation, it may actually form an important part of a much larger system of organisms, and its disappearance could have far-reaching consequences. It is therefore essential that, for the sake of the environment, ecologists continue to identify and preserve keystone species.

❸ Now answer Questions 1–13 below.

Questions 1–7
The Reading passage has seven sections, **A–G**.

Choose the correct heading for each section from the list of headings below.

List of headings	
i	When human intervention is not a factor
ii	Testing the theory
iii	The dominance of carnivorous keystone species
iv	It's the small things that matter
v	Putting knowledge to practical use
vi	An argument that has divided the scientific community
vii	A wide variety of shapes and sizes
viii	Why bees are disappearing
ix	A man-made structure reflects nature
x	Re-examining an old case

1 Section A ....
2 Section B ....
3 Section C ....
4 Section D ....
5 Section E ....
6 Section F ....
7 Section G ....

Questions 8–11

Complete the sentences below. Choose NO MORE THAN THREE WORDS from the passage for each answer.

8 Scientists fear that, in the near future, the unexplained disappearance of honeybees will affect the ecosystem and have a major impact on ....

9 The arches on old buildings rely on keystones for their ....

10 A .... in the numbers of some species in Mukkaw Bay occurred following Robert Paine's removal experiment.

11 Kelp forests in the North Pacific have almost disappeared as an indirect result of .... falling.

Questions 12–13

Choose TWO letters, A–E.

Which **TWO** reasons does the passage give for dodos becoming extinct?

A Humans altered their natural habitat.
B Their eggs were eaten by European settlers.
C Other animals preyed on unborn birds.
D They were too slow to avoid hunters.
E One of their main food supplies died out.

Grammar

Speculating and talking about the future

Complete this passage with expressions from the box, depending on the certainty of the event (*certain, probable* or *improbable*).

a strong likelihood	bound to	~~highly likely~~
little likelihood	may well see	no doubt that
quite possible	unlikely to be	very little chance
very much doubt	will	

According to the latest research, it's **1** (*probable*) *highly likely* that by 2050 80% of the world's people will live in urban areas, and the population will have increased to over nine billion. Furthermore, it's **2** (*probable*) .... that people will be living much longer than they are now. Many experts say that unless drastic measures are taken, we **3** (*probable*) .... dramatic shortages of both food and arable land. If this happens, famine and ecological catastrophe are **4** (*certain*) .... result.

A possible solution lies in vertical farming, which basically involves growing crops and other foodstuffs in specially-built skyscrapers. This would increase food production and reduce the need for arable land. The idea is ingenious, and there's **5** (*certain*) .... vertical farms would solve many problems. This idea has been received so enthusiastically that experts believe there's **6** (*probable*) .... we will see the first vertical farms within five years.

Speaking personally, however, I believe there is **7** (*improbable*) .... of this happening. Vertical farms would be very expensive to build, and I **8** (*improbable*) .... whether people would be willing to invest in a project that may or may not work. There is **9** (*improbable*) .... a rush of people coming forwards to say 'Here's £100 million. See what you can do'. In other words, there's **10** (*improbable*) .... we will see vertical farms appearing until the world's food shortage has become truly desperate, by which point, it **11** (*certain*) .... be too late.

Writing   Task 1

❶ Match these creatures, A–F, with their category 1–6 below:

1 reptile ....
2 freshwater fish ....
3 mammal ....
4 aquatic mammal ....
5 bird ....
6 insect ....

2 Look at the Writing task below, and answer these questions:

1 How are the charts linked?
2 How many paragraphs would you write, and what would you include in each one?
3 What would you say in your overview?

The charts below show the result of a long-term survey carried out by an environmental group into local wildlife population figures.

Summarise the information by selecting and reporting the main features, and make comparisons where relevant.

Write at least 150 words.

Main reasons for wildlife population changes (2000–present)

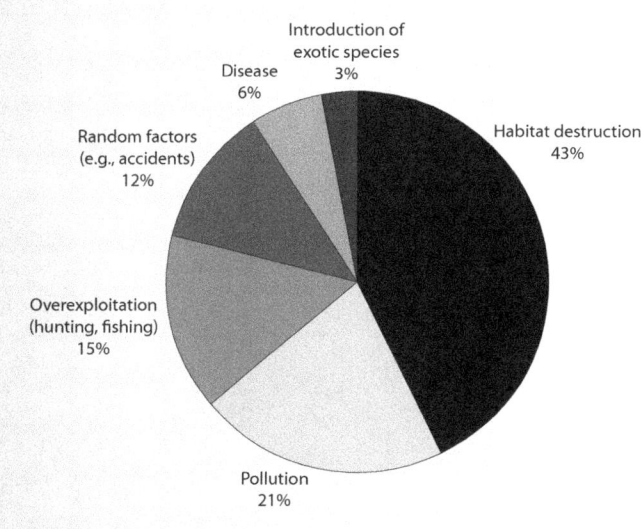

Percentage change in population figures for wildlife observed (2000–present)

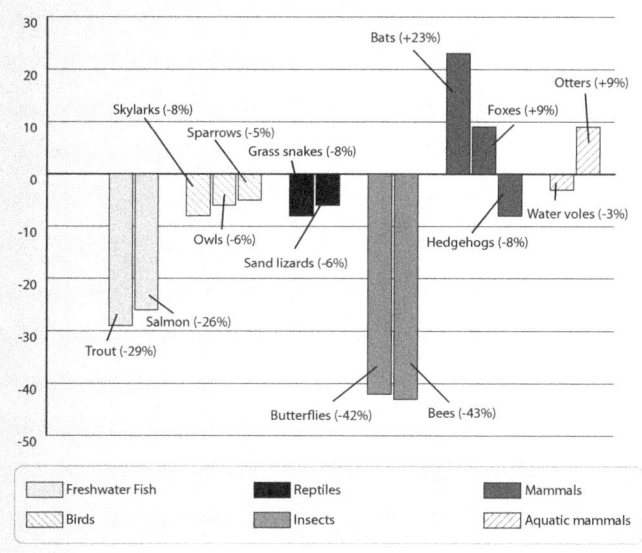

---

3 Here are four introductions from a sample answer. Which one is the best, and why? Why would the others not be suitable?

1 The charts show the results of a long-term survey carried out by an environmental group into local wildlife population figures from 2000 to the present.
2 The charts give information about wildlife in a particular area from 2000 to the present. The first chart gives reasons why wildlife figures have changed in the area, while the second chart looks at the wildlife which has been affected.
3 There are two charts. The first chart shows us why animal population figures are changing. The main cause is habitat destruction (43 percent). Other causes are pollution (21 percent), overexploitation (15 percent), random factors (12 percent), disease (6 percent) and introduction of exotic species (3 percent). The second chart shows which animals have increased or decreased in numbers. Most of them have decreased, but some have increased.

4 Here are some sentences from a sample answer. Each one is missing one or more commas. Insert the commas where you think they would be most appropriate.

▶ Student's Book, page 121

1 Although habitat destruction is the main cause for changes in wildlife population other factors have had an impact.
2 Pollution and overexploitation through hunting and fishing have played a significant role as have random factors such as accidents.
3 The figures for insects are particularly noticeable with drops of over 40% for both butterflies and bees.
4 Bird and reptile numbers have fallen but at a much lower rate.
5 On a more positive note some wildlife has actually increased during this period in spite of the problems listed in the first graph.
6 Overall despite population increases for some species there has been a downward trend for most of them.

5 Now write your own answer to the question. You should spend about 20 minutes on this task. You can either incorporate the introduction and sentences above into it, or use your own ideas.

Our relationship with nature

Unit 8 Across the universe

Reading   Section 3

1 You are going to read a passage about something called *terraforming*. Can you tell what this word means from the title and the picture in the article below?

2 Quickly read through the passage to find out if you were right. Can you think of any reasons why people would want to terraform a planet?

Life on Mars?

Terraforming may sound like something out of science fiction, but some believe it is possible to turn that fiction into fact.

As plans are slowly being drawn up for the first manned mission to Mars, many space travel sceptics are asking one vital question: why go there? Mars is a barren, desolate planet, and with its thin atmosphere and bitterly cold climate, it would appear to be completely unsuitable for human life. Above all, it is a very distant place, and getting there would be an enormous challenge. However, the planet might just hold the key to long-term human survival. With the Earth's population currently at more than seven billion and climbing, we may eventually be forced to look elsewhere in the solar system for somewhere to live. It is just possible that, contrary to photographic evidence, Mars may be more promising than it appears.

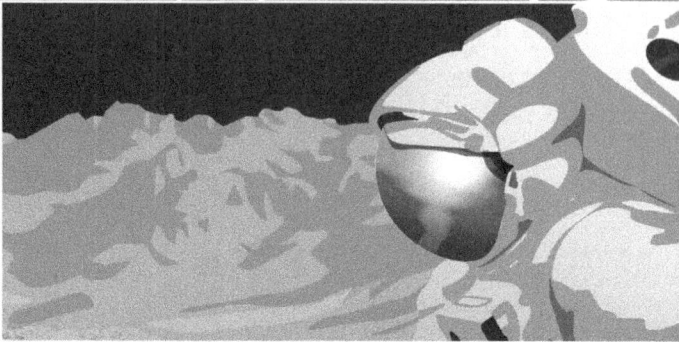

Today, Mars is a viciously cold, dry place. However, it does have some things in common with our own planet. For example, it has a daily rotation rate of 24 hours 37 minutes, compared with 23 hours 56 minutes on Earth. It also has an axial tilt of 24 degrees, which is just half a degree more than Earth's, and a gravitational pull one third of Earth's. Furthermore, it holds many of the elements that are required to support life, including carbon and oxygen (in the form of carbon dioxide), nitrogen, and frozen water at its polar ice caps. In fact, if you were to travel back in time several billions years, you would notice some remarkable parallels between the atmosphere on Earth then and Mars today. Back then, Earth was also a lifeless planet; until photosynthetic bacteria developed and began to produce enough oxygen to allow for the development of animal and plant life, our atmosphere also consisted entirely of carbon dioxide and nitrogen.

It comes as no surprise to learn, therefore, that some scientists believe the same process which turned Earth's atmosphere from mostly carbon dioxide into breathable air could be repeated on Mars, but by using technology rather than by letting nature and evolution take its natural course. Terraforming, as this process is known, would initially create a greenhouse effect that would heat the planet, which in turn would create other conditions necessary to provide a suitable living environment for plants and animals. However, it would be a highly challenging undertaking, and the process of terraforming the entire planet into an Earth-like habitat could still take many thousands of years.

Three terraforming methods have been suggested, with the first already under development, albeit for a different purpose. At present, the American space agency NASA is working on a system that will use large mirrors to capture the sun's radiation. This radiation will be used to propel spacecraft through space, removing the need for heavy and expensive rocket fuel. With a few changes, it might be possible to use similar mirrors to reflect the sun's radiation and heat the surface of Mars. Aimed at the planet from a distance of two hundred thousand miles, these enormous mirrors would raise the surface temperature by a few degrees. If they were concentrated on the polar ice caps, they would provide enough heat to melt the polar ice caps and release the carbon dioxide that is believed to be trapped there. Gradually, as the temperature rose, greenhouse gases would be released, and this would create a form of Martian global warming, the first stage in making the planet sustainable for life.

The second method would be to set up greenhouse gas 'factories' in order to raise the temperature of the planet. It is generally accepted that greenhouse gases produced by heavy industry are raising the Earth's temperature. Therefore, by building hundreds of greenhouse-gas emitting factories on Mars, a similar effect could be achieved. Carbon dioxide, methane and other greenhouse gases would be pumped into the Martian atmosphere. The same factories would then produce oxygen by mimicking the natural process of plant photosynthesis: they would inhale the carbon dioxide they produce, and then emit oxygen. The process could be accelerated by 'sowing' the planet's surface with photosynthetic bacteria, which would increase the rate at which oxygen is produced. Eventually, there would be enough oxygen on the planet for humans to breathe using only special apparatus similar to that used by mountain climbers.

The third, and by far the most extreme, method has been proposed by space scientists Robert Zubrin and Christopher McKay. They believe that it would be possible to produce greenhouse gases and water by firing large, ammonia-bearing asteroids at the planet. Each asteroid would weigh about ten billion tons, and would be powered by huge rocket engines which would move it towards Mars at over 10,000 miles per hour. At this speed, it would take each asteroid about ten years to reach its destination. The energy produced by one asteroid slamming into Mars' surface, say Zubrin and McKay, would raise the temperature of the planet by three degrees Celsius and melt about one thousand billion tons of ice at the polar caps. They believe it would take many of these asteroids, and at least fifty years, in order to create a temperate climate and enough water to cover a quarter of the planet's surface.

Terraforming Mars, if it is ever attempted, will be neither cheap nor easy. And it certainly won't be quick: although optimists like Zubrin and McKay say it could be achieved in five or six decades, the reality is that terraforming is more likely to take hundreds or even thousands of years. Furthermore, it will stretch human ingenuity to its limits, and will require levels of will and commitment that have rarely been seen before. The challenge of developing a habitable environment and bringing life to the cold, dry world of Mars is fraught with challenges, but it might just be one that saves the human race.

❸ Now look at Questions 1–14 below, then find the answers in the passage.

Questions 1–5

Do the following statements agree with the views of the writer in the Reading passage?

Write

YES *if the statement agrees with the writer's view*

NO *if the statement contradicts the writer's view*

NOT GIVEN *if it is impossible to say what the writer thinks about this*

1. Pictures of Mars suggest it might make a good place for people to settle. ....
2. Modern Mars and ancient Earth looked remarkably similar. ....
3. One method of terraforming could involve adapting technology that is already under development. ....
4. Greenhouse gas factories would provide enough oxygen for people to breathe without special equipment. ....
5. Terraforming Mars would be an extreme test of human skill and intelligence. ....

Questions 6–9

*Choose the correct letter, **A**, **B**, **C** or **D**.*

6. Which one of these factors suggests that Mars might be a good place for people to settle?
A It is not too far from Earth.
B It has no other life forms living there.
C It has a cool, dry climate.
D It has some similarities with Earth.

7 The first step in terraforming Mars would be to
A make the planet warmer.
B create a breathable atmosphere.
C find a suitable source of water.
D create a habitat for living organisms.

8 Special factories on Mars could be used to
A control the level of greenhouse gases.
B absorb excess levels of carbon dioxide.
C produce oxygen in a manner similar to plants.
D help grow essential bacteria.

9 What is the writer's main purpose in the passage?
A To explain why we need to terraform Mars.
B To illustrate the three processes required to terraform a planet like Mars.
C To consider how and why Mars might be terraformed.
D To demonstrate how straightforward it would be to terraform a planet.

Questions 10–14

Complete the summary using a word A–I from the box.

One method of terraforming Mars would be to **10** .... asteroids at the planet. Rockets attached to an enormous asteroid would propel it towards Mars, taking ten years to **11** .... the enormous distances required. The asteroid would **12** .... the planet with incredible force and **13** .... enough energy to **14** .... the planet's temperature. The result would be a temperate climate and lots of water from melting ice caps.

A cover	B create	C hit	D increase
E land	F drive	G power	H rise
I shoot			

❹ **Review your answers carefully.**

Listening   Part 4

❶ **You are going to hear a lecturer talking about health problems associated with space travel and living in space. Before you listen, consider:**
1 the sorts of health problems an astronaut might face
2 possible ways in which he / she might overcome these.

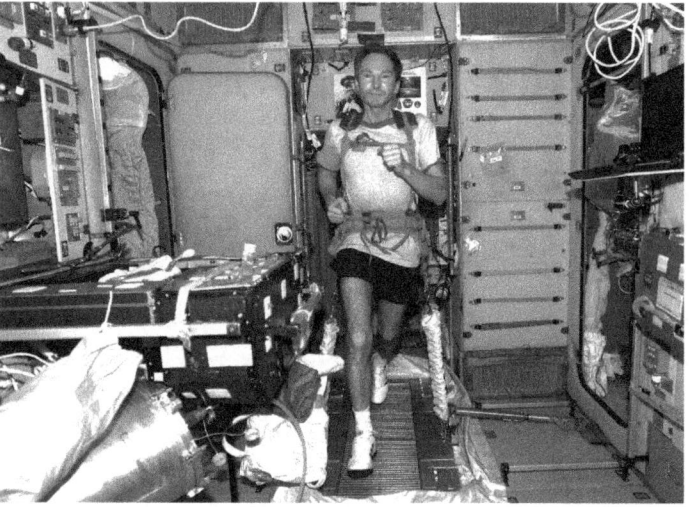

❷ **Look at the notes below and answer these questions.**
1 What sort of word or words (noun, verb, verb phrase, etc.) would you need to complete most of the answers?
2 Are there any answers you might be able to predict without listening to the lecture?

Questions 1–10

Complete the notes below.

*Write **NO MORE THAN TWO WORDS** for each answer.*

Space travel: health issues

Background

Crew on board ISS conduct **1** .... which establish effects of space travel on their bodies.

Findings: **2** .... of time in space have a negative impact on human body.

Effects on cardiovascular system

On Earth: human body can regulate **3** .... to compensate for effects of gravity.

In space: Amount and distribution is altered.

Results:
- Cold-like 4 ...., including headache and 'moon face'.
- Space motion sickness (affects roughly 5 .... of space travellers)

Effects soon wear off.

Effects on skeletal structure

Body loses calcium in zero-gravity situations:

Results:
- 6 .... reduced by about:
   3.2% after 10 days in space.
   2% per month thereafter.
- 7 .... become more likely.

Exercise reduces this risk and is also good for preventing loss of 8 ....

Effects of cosmic radiation

Big problem in space – can damage human DNA.

On Earth: people protected by a 9 ...., which prevents radiation reaching planet's surface.

In space: 10 .... of cosmic radiation can cause serious illnesses (including cancer, cataracts, brain damage).

3 🔊 **Now listen to the lecture and complete the notes, then review your answers. Make sure:**

- you have not used more than two words for each answer. ☐
- your answers make grammatical sense in the context of the sentence. ☐
- your spelling is correct. ☐

Vocabulary

Verbs and dependent prepositions

1 **Complete this article with *as, from, in, on, to* or *with*.**

It's travel sickness, but not as we know it

It's very difficult to focus 1 .... a job you're supposed to be doing when you're not feeling at your best. Even a mild headache can distract you 2 .... the work at hand. But the next time you're battling a cold at work, spare a thought for astronauts. They not only have to cope 3 .... all the challenges that space travel throws at them, but often have to do it under intense physical and psychological duress.

Space travel takes an incredible toll on the human body, and some of the effects can be extremely unpleasant. One common problem is that of 'Space Adaptation Syndrome' (SAS), often referred to simply 4 .... 'Space Sickness'. The combination of the erratic movement of the spacecraft and lack of gravity results 5 .... symptoms that are very similar to sea sickness, and about half of all astronauts admit 6 .... experiencing it. In extreme cases, it can prevent them 7 .... functioning properly. Many astronauts regard it 8 .... the single most unpleasant thing about space travel. When you consider they spend weeks or months locked into a tiny airtight container, unable to wash, eating bland food and subjected 9 .... a thousand and one life-threatening hazards, you get an idea of how bad it must be.

SAS is recognised 10 .... one of the major obstacles to overcome before commercial space travel (or space tourism as it is also known) is made available to the general public, and companies involved in space tourism programmes have spent a lot of time and money 11 .... finding a way to prevent it. Personally, I would love to take a trip into space, but I think I'll wait for them to come up with a suitable cure for SAS before I agree 12 .... get on a spaceship and be hurled into the inky depths of space.

Key vocabulary

2 **Complete each gap in this passage with one or two words from the box.**

allocated	ancient	civilisations	comet	cult
eclipse	following	galaxies	magnify	picture
solar (x2)	sustain	universe		

For 1 ...., space was a mystery and, as with all mysteries, people naturally wanted explanations. In most cases, they turned to the supernatural. Astrologers watched the movement of stars and planets to predict the future. Kings and emperors took the sudden appearance of a 2 .... in the sky as a sign that they would be victorious in battle. Priests warned everyone that a 3 .... was a sign the gods were angry. Many planets even had their own 4 ....

Across the universe

For the Romans, for example, Mars, Jupiter and Venus were astral representations of their most powerful gods, and they worshipped them accordingly.

Things have changed since then, of course. These days, we are able to study distant **5** .... using the most up-to-date equipment. Powerful telescopes on land and in space **6** .... planets, stars and **7** .... systems many light years away, and have helped us to build up a comprehensive **8** .... of space. Furthermore, thanks to rocket technology, we have started to physically explore our own **9** .... We have even started sending rockets to places like Mars to find out, among other things, if they might one day be able to **10** .... life. In some countries, huge amounts of money are **11** .... for the exploration and exploitation of space. In fact, space is no longer a mystery. It is big business.

Grammar

Emphasising

Complete the second sentence in each pair so that it has a similar meaning to the first sentence.

1 Apollo 11 went on the first moon mission, not Apollo 13.

It was *Apollo 11 that / which went on the first moon mission, not* Apollo 13.

2 Challenger was the first space shuttle, not Columbo.

It wasn't .... Challenger.

3 Many scientists think that asteroids contain lots of useful resources like iron ore and fossil fuels.

Asteroids .... lots of useful resources like iron ore and fossil fuels.

4 Space travel pushes human endurance and ingenuity to its limits.

What .... human endurance and ingenuity to its limits.

5 A lack of funds is the only thing stopping many countries from starting their own space programme.

All .... a lack of funds.

6 Specially selected journalists were the only people allowed into the mission control centre.

It .... allowed into the mission control centre.

7 The Apollo moon landings showed how much humans can achieve if they have sufficient determination and ambition.

What .... how much humans can achieve if they have sufficient determination and ambition.

8 Experts say light speed travel can be done, but I don't think it's possible.

Whatever .... , I don't think it's possible.

Writing   Task 2

❶ Look at the Writing task below, and underline the key words and phrases. Make sure you understand what you should include in your answer.

Write about the following topic.

As Earth runs out of natural resources, we have started to look to space for solutions. However, some people argue that this is the wrong thing to do, and instead we should look for alternative solutions here on Earth.

To what extent do you agree with them?

What alternatives might there be to exploiting space for natural resources?

Give reasons for your answer and include any relevant examples from your own knowledge or experience.

Write at least 250 words.

2 Focus on the first question in the task.

1. Decide which side of the argument you will take.
2. Spend one or two minutes brainstorming some ideas. Don't forget to brainstorm for both questions.
3. Incorporate your ideas into this tabled plan *in note form only* (do not write complete sentences).

Examples of natural resources we are running out of (1 or 2 examples)	
Possible reasons why we *should* or *shouldn't* look for replacements in space	
Alternatives to going into space for these resources	

3 Look at this introduction from a sample answer. In what way is this a good or bad introduction?

> Earth's natural resources are running out and, with a population exceeding seven billion and climbing, there is no doubt that they will soon be entirely depleted. Scientists predict that unless more resources are found soon, the human race will face some insurmountable challenges. However, I believe that looking to space for a solution is the wrong thing to do.

4 Order these sentences (1–5) from the second paragraph of a sample answer.

a) They suggest that we could mine asteroids for these resources, as they are thought to contain rich sources of fossil fuels similar to oil and coal. ......
b) Some scientists believe that we would be able to find suitable replacements in space. ......
c) Others think that we might find similar resources on some of Earth's nearest planets, like Mars and Venus. ......
d) Without them, we would not be able to power our industries, heat or cool our homes or drive our cars. ......
e) Take fossil fuels as an example of a diminishing resource. ......

5 Now do the same with the next paragraph.

a) It is true that eventually they would need to seek out alternative ways of bolstering their economy, but the short-term impact would be devastating. ......
b) Although at first glance this seems like a reasonable solution, there are three compelling counter-arguments. ......
c) Furthermore, there is the environmental argument. Do we really want to continue polluting our planet with fossil fuels? ......
d) Secondly, there is the economic impact it would have on countries which rely on fossil fuel exports as their main source of income. ......
e) First of all, space travel is extremely expensive, and it is doubtful the amounts invested in such ventures would pay off. ......

6 Using the notes you made in Exercise 2, write your own introduction and first two main paragraphs. Don't forget to state your point of view in the introduction.

7 In the next paragraph, the writer answers the second question in the task. Decide where sentences a–d would go in this paragraph.

1 .... 'Green' power (wind farms, solar power, etc) already exists, but is generally under-utilised. 2 ....
In most cases, this is due to economic concerns, as initial costs can be prohibitive.
3 .... At the same time, countries that rely on exporting fossil fuels for their main source of income should be helped to develop other industries. 4 ....

a) Perhaps what we need to do is give these countries loans or grants to develop these alternatives.
b) What alternatives there might be is an interesting question.
c) That way, their economies will not be adversely affected when their fossil fuel supplies eventually run out.
d) One problem is that while fossil fuels are still easily available, many countries are unwilling to invest in alternative energy technologies.

8 Complete the answer you started in Exercise 6 by answering the second question in the task and finishing with a suitable overview.

Recording scripts

Unit 1

Track 2

Alan Hello. Care for the Community. How can I help?

Philippa Oh, good morning. I'm interested in doing some part-time work for your organisation. Am I speaking to the right person?

A You are. I'm Alan Carpenter, head of human resources.

P Hello. My name's Philippa Tai…

A Hang on, sorry, let me just get a pen so I can take this down. OK, fire away.

P My name's Philippa Tailor.

A F-I-L-

P No, P-H-I-L- I-P-P-A.

A Got that. And is it Taylor with a y?

P No, an i. T-A-I-L-O-R. Like the job.

A Right. And what do you do at the moment, Philippa?

P I'm a student. I've just started my second, sorry, I mean, my third year at Brookfields University.

A Oh, right, what course are you doing?

P A BA in Social Care Studies.

A And have you got a number we can get you on?

P Sure, I'll give you my mobile. It's 0878 643 9884.

A 0878 643 9844.

P No, that's 884 at the end, not 844.

A Sorry. Right, what next? Oh yes, your email address, if you have one.

P I do. It's flipt14 at chatbox.co.uk. That's F-L-I-P-T, and the number 14, all written as one word. At chatbox.co.uk.

A Thanks. OK, and when would you be available to work? Days? Evenings?

P Well, days would be difficult, as I have classes then, so it would have to be evenings, I guess. I was thinking maybe a couple of evenings a week, or maybe three. But no more than that. Oh, and not Saturday or Sunday, if possible. Would that be any good?

A Oh, that would be fine. And would you be able to start immediately if we had anything for you?

P Yes, I would.

A Right, Philippa, so could you tell me why you're interested in working for us?

P Well, I'm hoping to apply for a career in social care when I graduate, and this would give me some work experience in this field.

A Any particular area?

P Yes, I'm particularly interested in helping young people, teenagers who have learning difficulties. You know, providing them with the extra care and support they might not get at school or home.

A And have you done anything like this before?

P Yes, in fact I've just spent the holiday working at a summer camp for children from disadvantaged backgrounds.

A Did you enjoy it?

P Oh, yes. It was challenging but rewarding. That's the sort of thing I like, really. And I'd like to do more of that, if possible.

A Great. And what makes you suitable for this kind of work, do you think?

P Well, I have very good communication skills. That's my strongest point, I reckon. And I'm a good listener. Sometimes you can help by just listening, you know?

A I agree. Hmm, right, what I'd like to do, if it's OK with you, is fix an appointment so we can meet and talk about this some more. It wouldn't be anything formal, not an interview or anything like that. Er, how are you fixed for Tuesday 9th September at 4.30?

P Ah, I'm sorry, I have a tutorial then. Would Wednesday be possible?

A The 10th? Yes, that would be fine. So we'll say Wednesday 10th at 4.30. Now, do you know where we are?

Unit 2

Track 3

Radio host Hello, and welcome to today's edition of Book Club. Later we'll be reviewing the latest novel by Lucy Armstrong, but first we're going to look at a new book which has been released to accompany the 'Colour my World' exhibition at the Science Museum. And Kirsten's here to tell us more.

Kirsten Indeed, good morning Jason. Well, it's called *Spectrum*, it's by Alex Mackenzie, and I must say it's one of the most interesting books I've seen for a long time. There are fifteen chapters, and each one looks at a different aspect of colour.

RH Can you give us some examples?

K Indeed. There's a fascinating chapter called *The hidden jungle*, which looks at the way an animal uses camouflage to conceal itself from predators, or make it invisible from other animals when it hunts them. By camouflage, of course, I mean their colour, shape, patterns on their skin and so on. This was a particularly striking chapter because of its amazing photography. Some of the animals are so well camouflaged that even when you know what you're looking for, it takes time to see the actual animal. So when you do finally find it, it's like an optical illusion.

RH Any others?

K Well, yes. There's a great chapter called *A question of choice*. Have you ever wondered why some people like colours that others don't? Why, for example, would some people never buy an orange car while others would pay extra for one? The question of colour preferences is answered here. Not surprisingly, it's all to do with personality and the things that we associate colours with. For some, orange is a positive colour, the colour of fire and flames. For others, the first thing they think about when they see the colour orange is, well, an orange. What I liked about this chapter was a test where you see pictures of things, er, cars, mobile phones, clothes and so on, in groups of ten, identical except for their colour, and you have to grade them in the order in which you like them, based on their colour. A key then analyses your personality based on your answers. This is popular psychology, of course, but the book also has some chapters devoted to serious science. One of these is called *It's all in the mind*. Now, you may or may not know this, but our eyes are like our fingerprints, nobody's are the same. Yet despite these differences, we all perceive colour in the same way. Light blue is always light blue, no matter how our eyes are structured. Why is this? Well, basically, it all comes down to the brain. To put it simply, our eyes just let in light, and our brains do the rest. The chapter explains in some detail how this happens, and describes a few experiments you can do at home to see for yourself how it works. It's fascinating stuff, and great fun too, of course.

Track 4

RH Now, I understand you found the last chapter of the book particularly interesting.

K Absolutely. The final chapter is all about the way colour influences us when we go shopping. I don't mean the colour of the things we buy, but the colours that are around us when we're buying them. You see, although we tend to think that it is the range of products that encourages us to spend time and money in a shop or other retail outlet, things like lighting, space and colour play equally important roles. Now, colours in shops usually fall into two categories: warm colours such as red and orange, which are what we could call 'exciting' colours, and calming cool colours such as blue and green. And these categories are believed to have different effects on the shopper. Warm colours not only give you more energy, but there is evidence that they can also stimulate or bring on hunger, which is why they're used so enthusiastically by fast food companies in and outside their outlets. On the negative side, if these colours are too bright, they can have a hurrying effect on shoppers, so good news for fast food outlets who want a fast turnover of customers, but best avoided if you want people to spend more time, and therefore more money, in your shop. Blue creates feelings of trust and security, which explains why it's a common colour in banks and other financial institutions, and customers associate the other 'cool' colour, green, with the environment. Which is why it's used in places like shops selling organic products or health food, and is also a popular choice for cafés and coffee shops.

RH And the chapter describes how different types of shopper respond to different colours, doesn't it?

K Right. Now, I'm an impulse shopper. I don't always know what I want when I go to the shops, but if I see something I like, I'll buy it. Research suggests that people like me respond better, that is, we're more likely to buy something when red is the predominant colour in the shop. Of course, our spending habits are not just limited to shops where red dominates, but it does help. Orange, by the way, can have a similar, although less pronounced, effect. Those on a restricted budget tend to respond well to light blue. However, for those on a really low income, with very little spending power, the colour where they feel most comfortable parting with their cash, appears to be pink. Consumers with plenty of money respond well in an environment where the predominant colour is purple. And that's not really surprising when you consider that purple is considered to be the king of colours.

RH Why's that?

K Ah, well, you'll have to get the book to find out. But I can assure you, it's really revealing stuff.

RH Great, thanks Kirsten. Well, moving on, there seems to be …

Unit 3

Track 5

Sara Hi, come in. I'm Sara. Welcome to Chorleywood Pharmaceuticals. It's Matt, isn't it?

Matt That's right. Thanks for agreeing to see me.

S You're welcome. I understand you're interested in the work we do here, right?

M Yes, I am. I'm doing some research into modern medicine for my thesis, and I was hoping you could tell me a bit about painkillers, give me a bit of background information, and so on.

S Sure, well, it's a huge area. Let's start by looking at the different types of painkiller we make here, and we'll take it from there. OK?

M Great.

S OK, well, here at Chorleywood, we produce five commercially-available painkillers, or analgesics as they're more correctly known, each one based on a different active ingredient. Those ingredients are paracetamol, ibuprofen, aspirin, codeine and morphine. I assume you've heard of them all.

M I have. I use paracetamol when I get headaches.

S Right, in fact it's the best all-round analgesic for things like headaches and most non-nerve pains. It's believed to work by controlling certain chemicals in the brain so we feel less pain. It's safe to take regularly for long periods, but overdosing on it can have very serious side effects, including liver failure.

M Right, I've heard that.

S Then there's ibuprofen. This is an anti-inflammatory, which means that unlike paracetamol, it directly targets the affected area or areas. Basically, it works by reducing swelling. So, if you've twisted your ankle, for example, and it's swelling up, ibuprofen will be very effective at reducing that swelling.

M Like in a sports injury, for example.

S Exactly. Which is why it's so popular with sportsmen and women. And alongside paracetamol, it's the painkiller that doctors recommend for children. The one disadvantage over paracetamol is that while you're taking it, you may get an upset stomach, because it has irritant qualities.

M Aspirin can affect you in the same way, can't it?

S Right. Aspirin is believed to work a bit like paracetamol, but with side effects similar to those in ibuprofen. A bit stronger, in fact, which is why doctors and pharmacists advise that you avoid giving it to anyone under 12.

M What about the others you mentioned? Codeine and morphine.

S Codeine is much stronger than the others, so it's usually diluted, that is, it's usually combined, with paracetamol in pill form. The problem with codeine is that it can cause dependency. In other words, your body comes to rely on it. So once you stop taking it, you may feel a little ill for a while. Nothing serious, just weak, shaky, that kind of thing.

M And morphine?

S Well, as you probably know, morphine is the most powerful analgesic available. It's strictly prescription-only, and even then your doctor will need to see you on a regular basis to check you're getting the right dose and to see how you're responding to it. It should only be used as part of a long-term pain management programme. It's highly addictive of course, and when you stop the programme, the after-effects can be extremely bad.

Track 6

M So, what's the most popular painkiller?

S That would be aspirin. In fact, almost 40 percent of the products we make here are aspirin based.

M It's been around for a while, hasn't it?

S Indeed. In fact, we could trace its origins right back to ancient Greece, about two and a half thousand years ago.

M Wow, I didn't know it went back that far.

S Well, obviously it wasn't known as aspirin then, and it wasn't in pill form. People took dried willow tree leaves, which they knew had an analgesic effect, and made them into tea, which they then gave to women during childbirth. Nobody really knew what was in the leaves that helped to ease pain until over two thousand years later, in, er, 1823, I think it was, when Italian scientists identified and extracted the active ingredient, salicin.

M Salicin, that's S-A-L, er

S S-A-L-I-C-I-N. And later, it was also found in a particular type of flower called the meadowsweet. That was in Germany in 1838. Then in 1853, French scientists succeeded in making a liquid form of salicin, which they called salicylic acid, but the patients they tested it on complained that it caused bad stomach pains.

M So, a bit counter-productive then!

S Exactly! However, in 1893, German scientists discovered that mixing a chemical called acetyl into the salicylic acid greatly reduced its irritating side effects. And then in 1897, the German pharmaceutical company Bayer developed a process for creating a synthetic version of this acetyl salicylic acid.

M Acetyl salicylic acid. That's quite a mouthful!

S Which is why they shortened it to aspirin. That year, they began testing their product on patients, and two years later, when these clinical trials were complete, aspirin as we know it now was launched onto the market.

M Well, thank you for the history lesson. That's actually really useful. I might be able to use some of that. Now, I read recently that aspirin …

Unit 4

Track 7

As part of our series of talks on the history of visual art, I'd like to talk today about three forms of ancient art: cave paintings, petroglyphs and geoglyphs.

Now, when we talk about cave paintings, we're usually referring to paintings on cave walls or ceilings, but we can also include paintings on rocks and other surfaces outside. We can trace some of these paintings to the Upper Paleolithic era, which is around 40,000 years ago, and most of them have a similar theme, that is, wild animals such as bison, deer, bears and lions. Humans, when they're shown, are almost always shown in a hunting context. Interestingly, human hands also feature, and abstract patterns are a recurring theme.

A variety of materials were used to create these paintings, probably chosen for their vivid colours. Red and yellow ochre were the most common, but other painting materials included manganese oxide and hematite. Charcoal was the principal material used for the outlines. In most cases, the paintings were made directly on the flat rock surface, but occasionally a silhouette of the subject was cut into the rock first. Paintings made in this way are generally much better preserved than others.

There has of course been much debate about why cave paintings were made. Were they simply put there for decoration, or did they serve a particular purpose? One theory suggests that images of animals were seen as possessing magic qualities, that painting them onto walls would increase the number of animals in the area and hence increase the food supply. I would dispute this, as while early humans would have wanted a ready supply of animals for food, this wouldn't explain why lions and bears are portrayed. There is, after all, no evidence that humans preyed on these animals. Quite the opposite, in fact – they would have done anything to avoid them! Perhaps one problem with working out why these paintings were made is that we're trying to understand the prehistoric mindset with a 21st-century mind. The simple fact, unfortunately, is that we'll probably *never* know why they're there.

OK, onto petroglyphs. These are images cut or carved into vertical or horizontal rock surfaces, and are mainly associated with prehistoric people going back about 12,000 years. However, some tribal societies continued making them for much longer, often until contact was made with more advanced cultures in the 20th century. In terms of subject matter, petroglyphs usually consist of geometric designs, but animals and people also feature. As with cave paintings, we're not sure why they were put there, but they may represent some kind of not-yet-fully understood symbolic or ritual language. What we do know is that even now they have a deep cultural significance for the descendants of the people who made them.

What is particularly interesting about petroglyphs is the similarity of designs across different continents. How could this be, when the people who made them could not possibly have come into contact with one another? One theory suggests that the similarities are a result of the genetically inherited structure of the human brain. Many of the geometric patterns, known as form constants, which recur in petroglyphs have been shown to be "hard-wired" into the human brain; they frequently occur in visual disturbances and hallucinations.

Geoglyphs are drawings or motifs on the ground, and are made either by arranging stones, stone fragments, rocks and gravel, etcetera on the surface to create positive geoglyphs, or by removing the top layer of ground to expose the rock beneath, creating a negative geoglyph. Size-wise, they're large, at least four metres across, and appear in various places around the world. The most famous are perhaps those in the Nazca Desert, a high arid plateau in Peru. These Nazca Lines, as they are known, were created about two and a half thousand years ago, and consist of hundreds of individual figures representing creatures, er, like birds, spiders, monkeys and lizards. What is particularly interesting is that, because of their size and position, these figures can only really be identified from the air. So, assuming the people who put them there couldn't fly, why make something that nobody could see?

Unit 5

Track 8

Claudia Hi, Dave. How are you? I tried calling you last night, but your phone was off.

Dave Oh, hi Claudia. Sorry about that, but I went to a talk by Professor Brian Jeffcott. You know, the guy who does those archaeology programmes on television.

C Oh, him. I think he's great.

D Me too. What I like about him is that he's the complete opposite of how you imagine these archaeology types to be, you know. He's young, funny, loads of energy. And he's so passionate about his subject. He's the sort of person who can make even boring things sound fascinating. I wish all lecturers were like that.

C So, what was it about?

D Well, in the first part of the talk he explained that researchers have recently discovered when Neolithic structures were built. You know, stone circles, hill forts, places where people lived and worked, that kind of thing.

C But I thought they already knew that.

D Sort of, but until now they only had a *rough* idea of when these structures went up, usually to within a few hundred years. But Professor Jeffcott showed us how new carbon-dating techniques and advanced computer programmes are allowing them to narrow that down to within ten or twenty years. And it's led to an interesting conclusion, which formed the second part of his talk.

C Which is?

D The research team generally assumed that Neolithic structures were built over a period of two or three thousand years. However, they now know that most of them went up over a 75-year period, about five and a half thousand years ago. And that's important because it means that they now have a more precise idea of when people went from being nomadic, that is, wandering from place to place, to being more static.

C Staying put, building permanent settlements, that kind of thing?

D Exactly. People only really build when they're settled. And that meant that their lifestyle altered in other ways. They went from being hunter-gatherers to being farmers. They started growing cereals, grains, that kind of thing. Well, the researchers knew that already, but what was news to them was how quickly Neolithic people took to other things at the same time. Within just a few years they learnt how to make pottery, domesticate animals, build timber houses, all sorts of things. They'd always assumed that these were developed over hundreds, thousands of years.

C Well, that's all fascinating stuff, but you're studying architecture. Why the interest?

D Ah, well, next week my class is going on a field project to look at prehistoric construction methods. We want to find out if they have any relevance today, you know, if ancient methods can be applied to modern structures. And then I'll be using that as the basis for my dissertation. So, we'll be visiting the Knowles Hill project. Heard of it?

C That's the place where they've reconstructed an entire Neolithic village, isn't it? It was on TV a few weeks ago.

D That's the one.

Track 9

D Anyway, what I need to do next is find out more about the period, get a bit more background information.

C Well, we can do that now. Let's see. Neolithic period, er, history, OK, there are loads of websites. Let's try this one. Oh, this lists key moments in, and features of, the Neolithic period in Britain. Any good?

D I guess so.

C So, the Neolithic period, which occurred towards the end of the Stone Age, started approximately 9,000 years ago, and lasted for about 5,000 years. At first, people lived in nomadic tribes, and wandered throughout Europe hunting and gathering.

D Nothing I didn't know already, unfortunately.

C Ah, but about 8,000 years ago, Britain became separated from mainland Europe when the sea covered low land between what is now England and France. That must be pretty important.

D Hmm, so people couldn't get back to mainland Europe. Which could mean they started evolving differently, socially and culturally, that is.

C It doesn't say, but it does tell us that between five and six thousand years ago, they started building houses that were permanent rather than temporary, which indicates they were becoming more settled. A connection, do you think?

D Possibly. What else?

C Other solid structures started appearing. Stone circles like Stonehenge, for example. Actually, that came a bit later, about four thousand five hundred years ago. Oh, it says here that it was built in several different stages over many hundreds of years. I didn't know that. I'd always assumed it all went up at once.

D Me too. That is interesting.

C OK, and this was also the time when pottery was first used to make bowls and cups. And tools made from stone for building and farming became more sophisticated. *And new agricultural techniques also appeared.* Wow, they were busy!

D They certainly were. Does it say anything about why …

Unit 6

Track 10

Today, as part of our series on e-commerce, I'm going to tell you a bit about internet banking, or online banking as it is also known, and how it has developed over the years.

Now, believe it or not, online banking actually began way back in the early 1980s, before we even had the Internet. Anyone who had a computer terminal and a monitor could access the banking system through their phone line. Services were extremely basic, compared to those today. You could view your statements online, and you could also send messages to your bank, but that was about it. If you wanted to transfer money or pay a bill, you had to send written instructions to your branch. Anyway, the first banks to offer this service were in the USA in 1981, and the idea soon caught on in other countries, arriving in the UK in 1983. As you might expect, however, the number of people using these services was very small, probably less than one percent of all account holders, and most of those were businesses.

This all started to change in the 1990s, when the Internet took off. More and more people were buying personal computers and going online, and in 1994 some financial institutions started implementing online banking services through a web browser, like they do today. Of course, many consumers were hesitant to conduct transactions over the Internet. They thought it was unsafe, and not without reason, as the large number of online thefts from that time can testify. As a result, customer numbers remained relatively low. However, two things gradually changed public attitudes. The first was that banks spent a lot of time and money improving security features for their websites. The second was the sudden increase in online stores, er, such as Amazon and eBay. As the idea of paying for items online became widespread, people began to feel more comfortable conducting financial transactions over the Internet.

Suddenly, internet banking really became popular. In 2001, for example, the Bank of America became the first bank to top three million online banking customers, who between them that year made over three million electronic bill payments worth over a billion dollars. By 2012, an estimated 62 percent of account holders in the US and UK were using online banking services. In some countries, Sweden being one example, up to 90 percent of bank customers were doing it. In the same period, a lot of online banks, that is, those banks which *only* existed on the Internet, came into existence, offering better interest rates and more services.

So what's the attraction? Online banking has many advantages for the customer, of course. They can view their accounts 24 hours a day, 7 days a week, they can pay their utility bills, or most other bills for that matter, transfer money, arrange loans and so on, all without leaving the comfort of their own homes. In fact, with today's smart phones, they don't even need to be at a computer to do all of this. But how do the banks benefit? Well, research has shown that, compared with offline customers, those who use online banking tend to maintain higher balances. They also require less support, by which I mean they ask for help less frequently, which helps banks to cut down on staff. They are also less likely to switch to or use another bank. Interestingly, they're also more likely to recommend their bank to friends and family. Banks which are purely online also have the advantage of not having to maintain the expenses of traditional bank buildings. Things like rent, building maintenance, staff, and so on. Furthermore, banks with a strong regional identity, such as Ulster Bank in Northern Ireland, have been able to use internet banking to expand their customer base beyond their original territory. In other words, you no longer need to live in Northern Ireland to hold an account with them.

Unit 7

Track 11

Student Morning, Professor Blake. Can I have a word?

Tutor Good morning, Ewan. Come in and take a seat. What can I do for you?

S Well, at the weekend, I'm going to be doing a survey on birds in the Wychwood nature reserve …

T As part of your project on endangered British species, right?

S Right. The thing is, I've never done this before, and as you're a keen birdwatcher, I was wondering if you had any useful tips.

T OK, sure. Well, the first thing you should do is get yourself a good pair of binoculars. They should be as light as possible so they're not uncomfortable around your neck, and their optical quality should be very good. You don't want to come back from your trip with eye and neck strain, after all.

S Definitely not!

T Now, the most important thing to do is to practise good fieldcraft.

S Fieldcraft?

T Right. You need to think like a hunter and stalk the birds carefully. Be slow and patient and avoid sudden movement. Don't wear bright clothing, or clothing that rustles. And try to avoid talking or even whispering loudly, as this is guaranteed to scare the birds off. If at all possible, you should also try to camouflage yourself against the background, and keep below the skyline, to avoid being seen by the birds.

S What about identifying the birds?

T Well, some people take a guide book with them, but they then spend the whole time with their nose buried in it rather than watching the birds. My advice is to leave the actual identification of the bird until last.

S OK, so what should I do?

T Well, once you've spotted a bird, start by listening to its call or song. This is one of the best bird identification tools there is. You then need to use visual clues, so start with an assessment of the bird's overall appearance. What is the approximate size of the bird? It's easiest to estimate the size in relation to birds you already recognise.

S So, for example, it's bigger than a blackbird but smaller than a pigeon.

T That's the idea. You also need to look for facial markings and bill characteristics. And also look out for other distinctive markings, especially on its wings.

S Not particularly easy, I guess, if the bird is flying around a lot.

T That's true, but the way a bird moves can also help you to identify it, er, how it walks, for example, or how it moves from branch to branch in a tree. And how does it fly? Are there any patterns there?

S Like, does it glide gently and steadily with each wing beat, or does it swoop up and down in gentle arcs?

T Exactly. Then try to determine its feeding habits. Not only what the bird is eating, but also *how* it feeds. And don't forget its preferred habitat is important too. Each species of bird has a typical region that they inhabit. Anyway, when you've finished observing one bird, but before moving on to another, make notes about your observations. You could even make rough sketches of the birds you see. And finally, at the end of the day, when you're back home, …

S Look up the birds in my guide book.

T Right!

Track 12

T Now one of the good things about the Wychwood reserve is that it has several hides where you can observe the wildlife. Have you got a map of the reserve?

S I have.

T Great, I can show you where the best ones are. OK, so, you've got the entrance to the reserve, here in the south, and there's the sea to the north. Now, there are several hides, and each one is named after a different bird.

S OK.

T The best ones are Goose hide, Eagle hide and Cuckoo hide. So, let's start with Goose hide. This is the best place for spotting water birds, er, freshwater birds, that is. On your map can you see a lake on the right, beyond the woods by the entrance?

S I've got it.

T There are two hides there, and Goose hide is the one on the far side. It's better than the other one by the lake because it's hard up against the hill behind it, which helps to camouflage it slightly. No skyline, you see. And you can get to it by taking one of the paths around the lake. The one running anti-clockwise is shorter but it's a bit marshy, so you might want to go the longer way, which takes you around the north side of the lake.

S Right.

T To get to Eagle hide, which will give you the best opportunity to see birds that frequent hills and mountains, follow the same path from the entrance and around the north side of the lake, but turn left where the path forks, shortly before the bridge over the stream. Then head towards the sea. You'll find Eagle hide where two paths meet. You'll get some great views of the hills on either side.

S Great. What about woodland birds?

T You've got a few options here, but like I said, Cuckoo hide is the best one. See the wood in the west of the reserve? The larger of the two on that side?

S Uh-huh

T That's where you'll find Cuckoo hide. It's on a raised platform, so you're right up in the trees with the birds.

S That sounds great.

T Right, well, good luck. I look forward to hearing how you get on. Are you going on your own?

S No, I've managed to persuade a friend to come along with me.

T That's good. It's much more fun when you've got company. And of course two pairs of eyes are better than one. Also, check the weather forecast before you go, because it won't be a very enjoyable experience if you find yourself walking around the reserve in the pouring rain. Oh, and don't forget there aren't any restaurants or cafés in the reserve, so it might be a good idea to pack something to eat in your bag alongside your binoculars. Go for something you can prepare before you go. Sandwiches, or something like that.

S Well, thanks for the advice. I'm really looking forward to it.

Unit 8

Track 13

As we inch closer to the reality of sending astronauts to more remote areas of our universe, with the proposed Mars mission receiving particular attention, I'd like today to look at some potential problems we may face living and travelling in deep space.

Now, you've probably all heard of the ISS, the International Space Station, but you may not know exactly what goes on there. The ISS is the world's first permanent orbiting research facility, and its main purpose is to perform the sort of scientific research that can only be carried out in space. Among other tests, the astronauts and scientists on board take part in medical experiments on themselves to determine how human bone and tissue is affected by living in a low or zero gravity atmosphere for long periods of time. And this raises one of the biggest problems of space travel – its effects on the human body. And you probably won't be surprised to hear they've found out that space travel can affect us in several ways physiologically, especially over extended time periods.

Let's start with its effect on the cardiovascular system. Now, living on Earth, we are affected by gravity because for two-thirds of the day we are standing or sitting. Because of this, body fluids such as blood pool in the lower part of the body. The human body is equipped with various mechanisms to oppose gravity to maintain sufficient blood flow to the brain. However, in an environment where there is minimal gravity, often called a micro-gravity environment, the quantity and distribution of body fluid alters, since it is free of the gravitational effect. This is known as 'fluid shift'. Its symptoms include a blocked nose, headache and a puffy face often known as 'moon face'. Similar to what you might experience during a heavy cold, in fact. This can also lead to space sickness. If you've ever been on a ship in stormy weather, you've probably experienced something similar. A few minutes or a few hours after entering weightlessness, astronauts experience headaches, nausea and a strong feeling of lethargy. About a half of all astronauts experience these symptoms, but they're short-term, and usually wear off after a few days.

This, unfortunately, is more than can be said for the effects that space travel has on the skeletal structure. Bones, of course, contain calcium and phosphorous, er, there are about 1,200 grams of calcium and 450 grams of phosphorous in the average human body. The problem with space travel is that once gravitational stress is removed, the body starts losing calcium at an alarming rate. In fact, after ten days of weightlessness, the body loses about 3.2% of its bone content, and then about 2% for every subsequent month spent in zero gravity, This weakens bones, which greatly increases the risk of fractures. The good news, however, is that it's possible to take countermeasures to minimise calcium loss. Basically, this involves getting plenty of exercise, which is why space stations are equipped with things like treadmills and exercise bikes. Incidentally, this also helps retain muscle strength. You don't use your muscles much in space, so they tend to weaken rapidly.

The biggest problem, though, is that of cosmic radiation, and this is the one that scientists are really struggling to mitigate. Cosmic radiation consists of fast-moving elementary particles, er, protons, electrons and stripped-down atomic nuclei. Nobody is certain where many of these come from, but there are theories that they originate in black holes or quasars, that is, distant galaxies producing large amounts of energy. When these particles hit human beings, they pass right through them, seriously damaging their DNA as they do so. On Earth, a magnetic field shields humans, deflecting the radiation before it can penetrate to the Earth's surface. However, without this shield, astronauts are exposed to dangerous levels of these high-velocity particles, and the further they go, the more they are exposed to them. The symptoms would be particularly unpleasant, with cancers, cataracts and brain damage heading the list of a whole range of medical conditions caused by radiation poisoning.

OK, so much for health. Now, let's consider the logistical problems of …

Acknowledgements

The author would like thank Judith Greet, Lynn Townsend and everyone else involved in the preparation of this workbook for their invaluable help, advice, suggestions and encouragement.

The authors and publishers acknowledge the following sources of copyright material and are grateful for the permissions granted. While every effort has been made, it has not always been possible to identify the sources of all the material used, or to trace all copyright holders. If any omissions are brought to our notice, we will be happy to include the appropriate acknowledgements on reprinting.

Guardian News & Media Limited for the text on pp. 8–9 adapted from 'University of Life' by Katherine Demopoulos, *The Guardian* 11/08/2006. Copyright © Guardian News & Media Ltd 2006; *The Independent* for the text on pp. 12–13 adapted from 'An invention to dye for' by Jonathan Brown and Steve Connor, The Independent 17/04/2006. Copyright © The Independent 2006;

Telegraph Media Group Limited for the text on pp. 20–21 adapted from 'Daily exercise significantly improves pupils test scores' by Graeme Paton, *The Telegraph* 09/03/2012 and 'Regular exercise can improve memory and learning' by Richard Gray, *The Telegraph* 19/02/2012. Copyright © Telegraph Media Group Limited 2012; Dr Yohannes Haile-Selassie and Cleveland Museum of Natural History for the text on pp. 32–33 adapted from '3.6 million year-old Relative of 'Lucy' Discovered: Early Hominid Skeleton Confirms Human-Like Walking is Ancient' *Science Daily* 21/6/10. Reproduced with permission of Dr Yohannes Haile-Selassie and Cleveland Museum of Natural History; Elsevier for the text on pp. 32–33(f) from 'Chimpanzee carrying behaviour and the origins of human bipedality' by Carvalho, Biro, Cunha, Hockings, McGrew, Richmond, Matsuzawa, *Current Biology* 20/03/12. Reprinted with permission of Elsevier;

Incisive Media/Business Green for the text on pp. 36–37 adapted from 'How Green is your PlanIT Valley' by James Murray, 28/06/10 www.businessgreen.com. Reproduced with permission.

Photo Acknowledgements

The authors and publishers acknowledge the following sources of copyright material and are grateful for the permissions granted. While every effort has been made, it has not always been possible to identify the sources of all the material used, or to trace all copyright holders. If any omissions are brought to our notice, we will be happy to include the appropriate acknowledgements on reprinting.

p. 6: © David Grossman / Alamy; p. 8: © Jeff Greenberg / Alamy; p. 10: © 67photo / Alamy; p. 13: Science Photo Library; p. 16 (TL): Shutterstock/Alekcey; p. 16 (BL): Shutterstock/Maks Narodenko; p. 16 (TR): Shutterstock/Buturlimov Paul; p. 16 (BR): Shutterstock/razihusin; p. 18 and 44 (UCL): Thinkstock; p. 20 (B): © By Ian Miles-Flashpoint Pictures / Alamy; p. 20 (T): © Dmitriy Shironosov / Alamy; p. 24 (R): Courtesy of The Advertising Archives; p. 26 (TL): jarnogz/iStock/Getty Images Plus/Getty Images; p. 26 (CL): Robert Harding/Getty Images; p. 26 (BL): © Nickolay Khoroshkov / Alamy; p. 26 (TR): © World History Archive / Alamy; p. 26 (BR): © Tetra Images/Getty Images; p. 28 (L): © Jon Helgason / Alamy; p. 28 (R): Stuart Clarke/Rex Features; p. 34: © Sabena Jane Blackbird / Alamy; p. 38: © Robin Beckham / BEEPstock / Alamy; p. 40: © Rosemary Roberts / Alamy; p. 41 (TL): Diego Cervo/Blend Images/Getty Images; p. 41 (TR): © Jim Holden / Alamy; p. 41 (B): © Richard Sheppard / Alamy; p. 42: © Paul Thompson Images / Alamy; p. 44 (TL): Hiroya Minakuchi/Minden Pictures/FLPA; p. 44 (TR): Photo Researchers/FLPA; p. 44 (UCR): Justin Lewis/The Image Bank/Getty Images; p. 44 (BCL): © Christina Wilson / Alamy; p. 44 (BCR): Sami Sarkis/Photodisc/Getty Images ; p. 44 (BL): Nature Picture Library/Simon Colmer; p. 44 (BR): Tom Shower/EyeEm/Getty Images; p. 46 (L): © Philip Sayer / Alamy; p. 46 (Photo A): Wil Meinderts/FN/Minden/FLPA; p. 46 (Photo B): FLPA; p. 46 (Photo C): Nature Picture Library/Kim Taylor; p. 46 (Photo D): Nature Picture Library/Chris Shields (WAC); p. 46 (Photo E): Murray Cooper/Minden Pictures/FLPA; p. 46 (Photo F): Nature Picture Library/Niall Benvie; p. 50: NASA/Science Photo Library; p. 52: © The Art Archive / Alamy.

Shaftesbury Road, Cambridge CB2 8EA, United Kingdom

One Liberty Plaza, 20th Floor, New York, NY 10006, USA

477 Williamstown Road, Port Melbourne, VIC 3207, Australia

314–321, 3rd Floor, Plot 3, Splendor Forum, Jasola District Centre, New Delhi – 110025, India

103 Penang Road, #05–06/07, Visioncrest Commercial, Singapore 238467

Cambridge University Press & Assessment is a department of the University of Cambridge.

We share the University's mission to contribute to society through the pursuit of education, learning and research at the highest international levels of excellence.

www.cambridge.org
Information on this title: www.cambridge.org/9781009683678

© Cambridge University Press & Assessment 2009

This publication is in copyright. Subject to statutory exception and to the provisions of relevant collective licensing agreements, no reproduction of any part may take place without the written permission of Cambridge University Press & Assessment.

First published 2004
Second Edition 2009

20 19 18 17 16 15 14 13 12 11 10 9 8 7 6 5 4 3 2 1

Printed in Great Britain by CPI Group (UK) Ltd, Croydon CR0 4YY

A catalogue record for this publication is available from the British Library

Library of Congress Cataloging-in-Publication Data
Richards, Jack C.
Connect / Jack C. Richards, Carlos Barbisan, with Chuck Sandy. – 2nd ed.
   p.   cm.
Summary: "Connect is a four-level, four-skills American English course for young adolescents. Connect encourages students to connect to English through contemporary, high-interest topics and contexts, fun dialogs, and games. Each student's book includes grammar and vocabulary presentations and a multi-skills, graded syllabus" – Provided by publisher.
ISBN 978-1-009-68367-8 (Student's bk. 1)
1. English language – Textbooks for foreign speakers. I. Barbisan, Carlos.
II. Sandy, Chuck. III. Title.
PE1128.R4553   2009
428.2'4–dc22
2008037556

ISBN	978-1-009-68367-8	Student's Book 1 (English)
ISBN	978-0-521-73698-5	Workbook 1 (English)
ISBN	978-0-521-73702-9	Teacher's Edition 1 (English)

Cambridge University Press & Assessment has no responsibility for the persistence or accuracy of URLs for external or third-party internet websites referred to in this publication, and does not guarantee that any content on such websites is, or will remain, accurate or appropriate. Information regarding prices, travel timetables, and other factual information given in this work is correct at the time of first printing but Cambridge University Press & Assessment does not guarantee the accuracy of such information thereafter.

Art direction, book design, photo research, and layout services: Adventure House, NYC
Audio production: Full House, NYC